S... ...D RUN A

...lu...ty Salon

Visit our How To Website at www.howto.co.uk

At www.howto.co.uk you can engage in conversation with our authors – all of whom have 'been there and done that' in their specialist fields. You can get access to special offers and additional content but most importantly you will be able to engage with, and become a part of, a wide and growing community of people just like yourself.

At www.howto.co.uk you'll be able to talk and share tips with people who have similar interests and are facing similar challenges in their lives. People who, just like you, have the desire to change their lives for the better – be it through moving to a new country, starting a new business, growing their own vegetables or writing a novel.

At www.howto.co.uk you'll find the support and encouragement you need to help make your aspirations a reality.

You can go direct to www.start-and-run-a-successful-beauty-salon.co.uk which is part of the main How To site.

How To Books strive to present authentic, inspiring, practical information in their books. Now, when you buy a title from **How To Books**, you get even more than just words on a page.

START AND RUN A

Successful Beauty Salon

A comprehensive guide to
managing or acquiring your own salon

Sally Medcalf and Bijan Yousef-Zadeh

howtobooks / **smallbusinessstart-ups**

Published by How To Books Ltd
Spring Hill House, Spring Hill Road,
Begbroke, Oxford, OX5 1RX, United Kingdom
Tel: (01865) 375794 Fax: (01865) 379162
info@howtobooks.co.uk
www.howtobooks.co.uk

How To Books greatly reduce the carbon footprint of their books by sourcing their
typesetting and printing in the UK.

British Library Cataloguing in Publication Data
A catalogue record for this book is available from the British Library

ISBN: 978 1 84528 376 6

Produced for How To Books by Deer Park Productions, Tavistock, Devon
Typeset by TW Typesetting, Plymouth, Devon
Printed and bound by Cromwell Press Group, Trowbridge, Wiltshire

NOTE: The material contained in this book is set out in good faith for general guidance and
no liability can be accepted for loss or expense incurred as a result of relying in particular
circumstances on statements made in this book. Laws and regulations may be complex and
liable to change, and readers should check the current position with the relevant authorities
before making personal arrangements.

CONTENTS

ACKNOWLEDGEMENTS

I would like to thank Bijan Yousef-Zadeh for inviting me to join him in the writing of this much-needed book. It was his encouragement and five years of persistence that finally persuaded me to take the plunge and put my thoughts and experience in writing. I do hope that all those who are planning to open their own salon or who already have one and read this book, will get the benefit of our experience and what we have offered, in their own beauty salons.

Sally Medcalf

For several years I have felt that there was a gap in the market for a book which could help the many beauty therapists who want to open a salon and those who already have one but want to improve it and make it more efficient and successful. My own knowledge and experience of business, sales and marketing management needed the expertise and experience of someone in the beauty industry and a beauty salon. And that someone, Sally Medcalf, who always insisted, 'But I just don't have the time', finally made the time to join me in creating this, what we believe to be a unique and informative book. The contents are based on nothing but real-life experience of our own successful businesses and we hope that those reading it will enjoy putting its many tips and suggestions into practice, while improving their beauty business prospects. I take this opportunity to say, 'Well done, Sally'.

I would also like to thank my daughter Bettina Hunt for spending many hours of her limited time proofreading the manuscript and making many constructive suggestions.

Bijan Yousef-Zadeh

PREFACE

The ever-increasing interest in all aspects of health and beauty has created an unusual demand for more shops, salons and spas offering beauty products and treatments. Women and men are maintaining their looks and caring for their appearance by going to beauty salons on a regular basis. As the demand increases all over the world, so does the number of people and beauticians who want to set up and run their own beauty salon.

The encouragement and support given by the government of the 1980s for people to become self employed, the many TV business programmes of the last decade, and the rapid expansion in computer technology, especially of the internet, have all contributed to a massive boost in the entrepreneurial spirit of thousands of people.

The appeal of working for yourself, being in control, experiencing the satisfaction of owning your own business, making decisions which directly affect your life, and looking towards a luxury lifestyle gained through your own effort has proved a strong lure. Unfortunately, having a good idea and the desire to start your own business is not enough to succeed – and the beauty industry is no different from all other businesses.

Experience shows that thousands of people who have a desire to be self employed and run their own business have neither the knowledge of where and how to start nor the tools to bring their dream to reality. Lack of understanding of the basics of running and managing a business and the reality of just how much hard work is needed to make the business a success, cause many new businesses to fail at the first hurdle and often within the first two to three years.

Although there are many seminars, short courses, lectures and television shows available which try to encourage and teach people how to start and run a business, there are very few which actually provide a step-by-step guide to starting and running a specialised business venture.

One of the most interesting aspects of the beauty industry is the fact that those who choose to study and make a career in this field have a passion for their work and love what they do. This is an essential ingredient for the success of any business. A love and passion for what you do, combined with proper guidance and informed advice, will greatly improve the prospects of you creating a successful business.

This book aims to provide that guidance and information. It was inspired by two very successful people who have spent most of their working lives self employed in various businesses, and in the field of beauty. The book includes hundreds of tips and recommendations drawn from their own experience and knowledge, providing you with a wealth of information to help you start and run your own successful beauty salon.

1
STARTING OUT IN THE BEAUTY INDUSTRY

The beauty industry is an exciting and rewarding one to be involved in. It is an industry which is expanding rapidly, with more people having regular treatments in hair and beauty salons, health clubs, spas and clinics. Many hotels now consider spa or beauty treatments to be an essential service to offer their guests. Beauty treatments are perceived as the perfect affordable antidote to our stress-filled lives, and looking your best is not a luxury any more but an essential part of a healthy lifestyle.

The one-to-one interaction with clients, the interesting conversations, the immediate satisfaction from doing a job well and making sure clients are relaxed and looking their best when they leave, give you a great sense of well-being. It is not surprising that beauty therapists and hairdressers come out top in work satisfaction surveys!

As you are reading this, unless you already have one, you must have decided to take the leap and start your own beauty business. But before we go any further, let's see if you have what it really takes to run a beauty salon and become a successful business person.

Should I own my own business?

To work for yourself and not for someone else requires a great deal of discipline, commitment, determination and self-reliance. You will have to make a lot of decisions on your own, which at times can be very stressful. For the first year or two you will have to work a lot harder and put a lot of hours into the business, with probably much less income. Owning and running your own business will require certain qualities and characteristics that are not common to everyone. So here are a few questions:

☐ Do you have a passion for beauty?

☐ Are you suitably qualified in the field of beauty therapy?

☐ Have you had at least two years' experience of working in a salon or spa?

☐ Do you consider yourself to be a hard-working person?

☐ Do you manage your time well?

☐ Are you self-motivated?

☐ Do you give up easily?

☐ Are you prepared to work long and unsociable hours, late evenings and weekends?

☐ Do you enjoy making decisions?

☐ Are you a risk taker?

☐ Are you a confident person?

☐ Can you work under pressure?

☐ Are you a good communicator?

☐ Do you have good health?

☐ Are you an optimist?

☐ Are you a good listener, and can you take criticism?

☐ Do you get stressed easily?

☐ Do you consider a setback as failure or as a learning experience?

☐ Do you enjoy being in charge?

☐ Are you a creative person?

☐ Do you prefer freedom and flexibility or routine in your working life?

☐ Are you an ambitious person aiming for financial success or a personal sense of achievement?

No doubt you already know what the answers to these questions should be. Most of the above questions and their answers are inter-related and are the ingredients or factors which help and contribute to the success of a person in business.

People often talk about entrepreneurs. An entrepreneur can be defined as an ambitious, self-motivated risk taker who is not afraid of failure. Do you see yourself as such a person? Obviously not every business person has the right answers to all the above questions, and some of them will have a range of answers and not simply a yes or no. But if you can easily see a lot of the above in yourself, then carry on reading this book – being self employed should work for you.

There are several ways of being self employed and running your own business. Your business could be operated as a sole trader, a partnership, a franchise or as a limited company.

SOLE TRADER

This means that you are self employed, the entire business belongs to you and you run the business on your own. You have the freedom of making your own decisions, working when you want and keeping all the profits for yourself. However, it leaves you with all the responsibilities of the business, it may mean no income when you are ill or go on holiday, and if you make any loss it will be all yours. You use your own name and possibly a trading name; for example, Debbie Howard T/A (Trading As) Beauty House.

PARTNERSHIP

A partnership will allow you to share the responsibility for decisions and the capital outlay but will also mean that you will have to share the profits. This is often the case for two or three people who cannot afford to start a business on their own, or have mutual interests and experience that will benefit the business. A partnership business is an excellent idea but very few last because of differences of opinion between the partners. If and when the partnership breaks up, it could seriously and adversely affect the business.

When a partnership is formed, you must ensure that a contract is drawn up outlining all the agreements and arrangements between the partners. Where possible, use a solicitor to draw up your contract or agreement.

FRANCHISE

When you choose to be a franchisee, you will get a licence to trade in the name of another company with an established and proven business. You will then get assistance and guidance with planning, layout and design of your premises, training and continuous support and management advice from that organisation. All of these will be under a well-known name, with a good reputation and successful track record. However, this will involve a large initial investment, annual payments to the company, and working within a set format and within the constraints laid down by the franchiser. In such a case you will have very little say in your new business – the format, design, or even the services or prices. They are all standardised and fixed by the company whose franchise you buy.

Today, there are an estimated 16,000 franchised systems operating around the world. Some are worldwide operations, and others are smaller regional companies. The main advantage of joining such a scheme and becoming a franchisee is that the business is generally already a proven success and the franchiser therefore has a vested interest in your own success, so you will receive all the help you need to operate your business responsibly and profitably.

LIMITED COMPANY

To run your business as a Limited Company (Ltd), you will have to be registered by the Registrar of Companies, a process carried out by your solicitor or an accountant. A Limited Company requires a minimum of two people as shareholders and usually starts as a private concern, but as it grows it can go public and sell shares and raise money for expansion. The main advantage of being a Limited Company is that the shareholders have a limited liability for debt. However, the disadvantage is that comprehensive annual accounts have to be prepared and submitted to Companies House and there are legal obligations for the company directors. You can buy a ready-made Limted Company (often referred to as *off the shelf*) or you can choose your own name and have it registered.

To decide whether your new business should operate as a Limited Company or not depends on your individual circumstances, turnover and profitability. It is best to discuss and get advice from your accountant on this subject.

How and where to start

Once you have made the momentous decision to start your own beauty business, you will have to decide what type of beauty business will suit you best. If you have never had a business of your own, it might be wise to start small and learn the tricks of the business before you take the plunge into the High Street. This could mean going mobile, working from home or renting a room in a hairdresser's salon. Each one of these has its own pros and cons.

GOING MOBILE

This is the most popular way to start out on your own in the beauty industry and requires minimal financial outlay. It is also popular with some clients; they often get a cheaper treatment, as the mobile business does not have the overheads of a High Street salon. Being constantly on the move, you should remember to maintain the high standards required of your profession, including cleanliness and sterilisation of implements. Also, don't forget professional insurance to include extra cover for accidents and mishaps in a client's home.

 Remember to change your car insurance to cover you for using your car for work purposes and to include the cost of your equipment in the car. It is a nightmare scenario to return to your car and find all your working tools gone. The British Association of Beauty Therapists and Cosmetology (BABTAC) and The Guild of Beauty both offer insurance policies for the mobile therapist.

Going mobile does not suit all beauty therapists. To run a mobile operation you must be:

☐ **Organised.** It is no use leaving at home that eyelash tint or vital spatula. To make sure you don't forget things, have a check list and use it. Before you leave home, be mentally and physically prepared.

☐ **Flexible and adaptable.** The mobile therapist must be prepared to work in any kind of situation and conditions, in a variety of people's homes. If you find it stressful to have the nail table at the wrong height or to do an airbrush tan in a cramped shower then a mobile business might not be for you.

☐ **Enterprising.** It will be down to you to generate new and repeat business.

☐ **Punctual.** You cannot afford to be late for your appointment for whatever reason. Your client will be sitting waiting for you.

 Make sure you have a reliable car, as your business is dependent on your transport.

THE PROS AND CONS OF GOING MOBILE

Pros

☐ Flexible working hours to fit around your other commitments.

☐ The initial financial outlay is quite low. Equipment can be built up slowly over time.

☐ Some people cannot leave their homes and need to be visited there.

☐ You will have no rent or overheads and very low running costs.

Cons

☐ You will be working unsociable hours such as weekends and evenings.

☐ Your income could vary a lot until you are well established.

☐ It can be difficult to find new clients particularly at the beginning.

☐ Business is very much dependent on you to promote treatments.

☐ Travelling around, parking, traffic jams and carrying equipment, especially in bad weather, could hamper your work and be physically exhausting.

☐ Travelling costs and special car insurance can add up.

☐ You will lose time travelling from one customer to the next and may have to charge your clients for it.

☐ Time lost in travelling results in fewer clients per day.

☐ Possible interruptions from children and other people in the client's house.

Keep all the receipts which are relevant to your work, including those for petrol, parking, car tax and repairs, etc. These will go in your accounts as your business expenses and will be offset against your tax bill.

WORKING FROM HOME

Using a spare room in your own home is another way of starting out. The advantage of this over going out to clients' homes is that you will have more control over the consistency of the treatments that you provide. You will have your own couch, trolley and room set up just as you like it, rather than adapting to what the client has available. Whether you are lucky enough to have a spare room which you could use exclusively for beauty or have a corner of your living room which you could partition off, with a little thought you will be able to create a peaceful space for providing beauty treatments. Although having a room exclusively for beauty use is not essential, always have a professional and clean appearance to the treatment area when treating clients. Keep pets and children away.

Keep all receipts for your heating and lighting. Your accountant will need these to offset a proportion of your household costs against your tax bill.

THE PROS AND CONS OF WORKING FROM HOME
Pros

☐ Flexibility to work the hours you want.

☐ No travelling or commuting to work.

☐ Very low start-up and running costs.

☐ Tax breaks for allowable heating, lighting and telephone expenses.

Cons

☐ There is no escape from work. Consider leaving the answerphone on when 'off' work. Or have a separate line or mobile just for business calls.

☐ Working from home can be lonely and isolating. Keep in touch with what's happening in the industry by going to trade shows and joining professional organisations such as BABTAC (British Association of Beauty Therapists and Cosmetology) or The Guild of Beauty Therapists for support.

☐ Not every client likes going to a therapist's house, especially if you live in a rural area or a difficult place to get to.

☐ Loss of space in your house.

☐ Limited time available for appointments as there will always be other things going on in the house which can restrict your work.

☐ Unless the room you use is confined to treatments only and has no other household furniture in it, it will not be considered very professional.

RENTING A ROOM

This is a more serious and professional option for working for yourself and running your own business. Renting a room in a hairdresser's premises or in a health club has the advantage that start-up costs are much lower than a High Street salon and usually most of the work on the building has been done already. If it is a complementary business to beauty, such as a health club or hairdressers, there will be a steady stream of potential clients to introduce to your services. Find out from your local council if they require a Special Treatment Licence for either the premises or the therapists and, if so, discuss with your landlord as to whose responsibility it is for acquiring this Licence. It is usually the landlord who will pay for and hold the premises licence, and your responsibility to hold a therapist licence (if required). Also, don't forget to obtain professional insurance (see Chapter 9).

Check who will be providing the equipment, such as couches and trolleys, products, wax and towels. Some landlords will provide everything for an increased rent or profit share. Others will provide just the room and leave it to you to provide everything else. This is an advantage if you have strong views on which products you like to use or which treatments you would like to offer. Although it will increase your costs initially, it is great fun to pick and choose what you want to use.

Financial arrangements vary and you should always get a second opinion from someone you trust, with regard to a fair rent. Sometimes paying a percentage of your income is a good way to start, as you will not be committed to paying a large rent at the beginning when you have few customers. The percentage usually varies from 30% to 60% of your income, depending on who pays for products, reception services, heating and lighting.

If the landlord's business is VAT (Value Added Tax) registered and they are taking payments for your services, ask if VAT is deducted from the amount payable to you. It might be worth your while to arrange for your clients to pay you directly by installing your own credit card machine and taking payments yourself.

Alternatively a fixed rent can work out cheaper if you already have an established clientèle. Do your homework and find out what is a 'fair rent' in your chosen area.

Make sure you get everything in writing by drawing up a simple contract clearly stating what is included in the rent, what is excluded, how the percentage of income is calculated, what is each side's notice period, and anything else that you have agreed, including any deposit.

THE PROS AND CONS OF RENTING A ROOM

Pros

☐ You will be able to gain new clients from the business that you are renting from, especially if it is an allied trade to beauty such as a dentist, hairdresser, beauty salon or gym.

☐ You will be able to work with other people rather than being isolated.

☐ You can get help and assistance from other people in the business.

☐ Your workplace will look and feel more professional.

☐ Hopefully you will have an established room which requires minimal alterations to meet required standards, and includes such things as a sink with hot and cold running water.

☐ You will have flexibility in your working hours to fit in with other commitments.

☐ Low start-up costs.

Cons

☐ You will have to work closely with colleagues who may have different professional standards from you, which can cause friction.

☐ It may be difficult to create your own 'image' for your business.

☐ Little or no control over opening hours and days.

☐ Very limited room for expansion of treatments and products.

☐ You will have to take responsibility for getting new clients by promoting yourself and your treatments.

☐ If you take time off you will not have an income but may still have to pay rent.

Remember to register with the Inland Revenue as self employed as soon as you set up in business. Keep a record of your income and outgoings, including receipts, in a simple accounts book which is available from most large stationers. Make sure you make a provision for tax which is payable half-yearly, not weekly as with PAYE (Pay As You Earn) contributions, by putting aside a proportion of your income into a savings account. The Inland Revenue tax return can now be completed easily online. However, you may want to seek professional advice from an accountant.

Opening a salon

To own and run your own beauty salon is obviously a major decision. It involves a great deal of research and planning, and there are many things to take into account. The following is a list of some of the most important things that need serious consideration:

☐ Should you rent a ready salon or buy an existing one?

☐ Should you buy the freehold of a building or buy the lease?

☐ Is it best to start fresh with an empty shop?

☐ Where would be a good place for your new beauty salon?

☐ How will you find the right shop?

☐ What treatments and what products should you offer?

☐ How will you price your treatments and products?

☐ How will you find and select the right staff?

☐ What equipment should you choose and where should you buy it?

☐ What about the design of the salon, decoration and colour scheme?

☐ What insurance do you need?

☐ How should you do the accounts and VAT?

☐ How much money will you need and where should you approach for extra finance?

The list is long and you are probably thinking, 'Where do I start?'

Every one of the above questions is important and contributes to the success of your business. Thinking about, preparing and carrying out all these things is part of running your own business, and, if undertaken correctly and properly, can be exciting and fun. The process needs patience, perseverance and your total commitment.

Go and look at other salons, study their locations, their names, the colour schemes they have used, their layout, and if possible see their treatment rooms. Have a treatment. It will give you a lot of ideas to incorporate into planning how you would like your salon to look.

The pros and cons of opening a salon

Pros

- ☐ You have control over your choice of premises, products, treatments and image.

- ☐ Bigger scope for expansion of treatments and the business.

- ☐ Much higher potential turnover and profit.

- ☐ You will gain a great sense of achievement from opening and owning your own salon.

- ☐ You will have the opportunity to demonstrate your potential and create a successful beauty salon.

- ☐ If properly managed, you will have more freedom to have time off, as the staff can run the salon and you will still have an income, unlike when you rent a room or are mobile.

Cons

- ☐ Your initial capital outlay and running costs will be much higher.

- ☐ You will be fully responsible for converting and maintaining the premises.

- ☐ There is a much higher financial risk.

- ☐ It is hard work and will require a lot of commitment from you.

Planning your beauty salon business

Planning your business is like planning a journey. You must know **why** you want to go, **where** you want to go, **how** you are going to get there and, when you reach your destination, **what** you are going to do. So it is wise to plan your journey.

Buying or renting new premises for your salon, designing the layout, getting the salon decorated, choosing the right furniture and equipment for treatment, employing staff, marketing and advertising your new business, and knowing how much money you will need and arranging the necessary finance will require a lot of time, effort and very serious planning.

It is therefore essential that before you do anything else, you draw up your *business plan*. Obviously, if you have never done one, you will not know where to start. So let's talk about it.

BUSINESS PLAN

To start a business, like anything else, it is essential to have a realistic working plan. A plan for your business, or business plan, is effectively a collection of your ideas, expectations for your business, how you are going to do things and your forecast of how things will go. It is in the form of a written document that describes your proposed business, its objectives, its strategies, the market it is going to be in and its financial forecasts.

Your business plan is not only very important and useful for you; it is a must if you are seeking financial support from someone or looking for a loan from a bank or even if you are selling your idea for a possible partnership. It is therefore very important that it is well thought out and carefully prepared.

It makes good business sense to prepare a detailed business plan when the idea of opening a beauty salon is still in the early planning stage, so that you can see if your idea is both worthwhile and financially viable. This is a very useful way of arranging your thoughts and ideas and all the information available to you on paper, thus allowing you to get an overall picture of the project.

 Make sure your business plan is realistic and functional. If you have no business experience, seek advice from people who do.

Talk to local commercial estate agents; look through local newspapers to get ideas about shops and the cost of buying one. Look at as many other salons as possible. Visit beauty trade shows and talk to potential suppliers; take notes and their details so that you can contact them when you are ready. Line up potential builders, electricians and other tradesmen. Search for suppliers of beauty products and equipment, and talk to them regarding your future needs: get ideas of what they offer, on what terms and at what prices. Talk to your local council regarding licences and see what their regulations are. You will need input and advice from all of the above in order to draw up a realistic business plan. Also, having made these investigations and fact-finding missions in advance, you will find things will go much faster and smoother once your finances have been sorted out and approved.

One very important aspect of having a realistic business plan is the fact that any potential investor in your business, or a bank that you may approach for a loan, will almost certainly base their decision on the strength of your business plan.

It is therefore very important that when you are preparing your business plan you should obtain and write down as much information as you possibly can and make sure that you include:

- **A good summary.** This is a synopsis of the key points of your business plan and should explain the basics of your business in an interesting and easy-to-understand manner. This part is very important as any potential investor or partner will get their feeling about your proposition from the contents and the way you have presented them. Take time and put thought into what you want to write, and if necessary get professional advice.

- **Your business proposal.** This is about your vision of your proposed business. It should explain why you want to open a beauty salon, what your business will offer to your potential customers and why you think there is an opportunity for your salon to succeed.

- **Your strategy for the business.** Here you should describe the premises and its locality, and your proposed opening days and times. Give detailed information about the products and treatments that you are proposing to use and the reasons behind your choices. Generally, explain how you intend to operate your salon.

- **Your sales, marketing and advertising plans.** Having found out about your competition, explain what impact they will have on your salon. Also write about your target customer base and how you are going to attract them to your salon. Explain how you are going to market your new salon and what types of advertising you propose to do, with details of the costs involved and your budget.

- **Your workforce.** This is about you and your staff. Write about your credentials and experience and what key skills you have to offer that will help your business succeed. Mention other members of staff that you intend to employ, including their expected skills and experience. Include your recruitment and training plan, time-scale and the costs involved.

☐ **Financial forecasts.** This is the most important part of the plan, particularly if you are going to borrow money to finance the business. This part of the business plan is where you translate what you have said about your business into actual numbers and should include:

1. How much capital you will need to get your business started.

2. What security and return you can offer your lender.

3. How you plan to repay any borrowings.

4. Cash-flow statements (and possibly graphs) for the first three years. The aim is to show that your salon will have enough working capital to survive the first months with the predicted income and rate of growth.

5. Profit-and-loss statements showing your estimated income, anticipated costs and expenditure, and your profit forecast.

 Try to cover several possible scenarios other than the one you are expecting. Remember sales of treatments and products may be slow or affected by seasonal or economic variations. Also, when you are making your forecasts, allow for the possibility of a delay of several months in the opening of your salon.

An example of a financial business and cash-flow forecast is shown in Chapter 9.

 When you are preparing your business plan, try to be realistic and honest with yourself.

CONTINGENCY PLAN

Like everything in life, things don't always go the way you planned them. You should also think about and allow time and money for possible problems and delays with such things as licensing, building work and decoration, legal matters, suppliers and stock. Have contingency plans in place so that you can deal with possible setbacks and delays. Include these contingencies in your business plan; they are what your potential financiers want to see, as they show that you are being realistic.

If you need further help on your business plan you should talk to your local banks. Most of them are very helpful to new and small businesses and often have a small business unit which can give you excellent advice. Their advice is often free because they want to have you as a customer and get your business. Another great source of advice is the government business website www.businesslink.gov.uk, an excellent up-to-date source of information on setting up your own business.

 Remember, lack of good planning is planning for failure.

2
THE SALON

The salon will be your business home. This is where your business life will start and grow; this is where everything in your business life will happen. So it is very important to get things right, from day one.

Choosing a location

People often wonder why shops on one side of the street thrive while on the other side they struggle to draw in customers. Every shopkeeper wishes they knew the answer to this eternal question. Here are some influencing factors:

LIGHT

A light and bright salon is always welcoming. If possible, it is good to have plenty of light coming through the window. This is particularly important in the beauty industry where customers want to see the 'true' colour of make-up or foundation. Good light is also important for doing manicures. You should consider placing your manicure table in the front window in order to draw in curious passers-by.

FOOTFALL

You should ensure that the premises are on a busy part of the road. Check if the pavement on one side of the road is busier than the other. Consider doing a count to see how many people actually pass your selected premises on any given morning or afternoon. Check to see if the road is a cut-through for traffic. The more people who pass or see your shop, the more potential customers you will have. It is obvious that a shop in a quiet or remote area will have less chance of success than one in a busy High Street or one with several other businesses nearby.

SHOPFRONT

Although there are many beauty salons doing well in basements or on upper floors, it is preferable to have your own door and windows. The potential for advertising your business is multiplied by the size of your window. Generally speaking, the larger the shopfront the more exposure and the better for trade.

LOCALITY

Local businesses, busy offices, universities or colleges, and hospitals are all potential sources of customers. If the local residents are your target clientèle, then make sure that the shop you find is located in an area with a lot of residential properties. Otherwise, ensure your salon has a good catchment of potential customers.

RIVAL BEAUTY SALONS

Don't be put off by other beauty salons in the area. Some competition is good for business as long as you can compete on service, value or unique treatments. In fact, customers going to other salons near you are a great source of potential clients, as they already have an interest in what you might offer. A lack of salons in the area might indicate that there isn't a 'need' for beauty treatment.

PARKING AND PUBLIC TRANSPORT

Another consideration when choosing the location for your new salon is its accessibility. Check for easy parking facilities near the salon. It will help if the salon is on a bus route or near a tube or railway station. This is important as difficult access or lack of parking often puts off potential clients. The easier it is to get to your salon, the more likely it is for people to come to you. This is also important for your staff as they too have to travel to the salon without too difficult a journey, particularly if they have to start early or finish late.

 Choose a location with lots of offices, day business, a college or university or even a hospital nearby. Don't rush; take your time until you find the right place, with the right terms and a good price.

Deciding on size

The size of your new salon will be determined by the amount of finance and resources available to you and the chosen location.

Before you even start looking at shops and suddenly fall in love with one and opt for a three- or four- or six-room premises, assess the area and the location, and accurately calculate your expenditure for:

☐ Setting up the salon (the amount of money you will need to refurbish and decorate and install equipment and all the necessary tools and products in every room).

☐ The amount you will need to keep running the business (cash flow) for at least six months to get established and get money coming in.

This is effectively your budget. In Chapters 8 and 9 we will discuss how to assess your finances and obtain a budget for your business. From your business plan and cash-flow diagrams you will be able to see how much you can afford for your business and what proportion can be allocated to the purchase of your new shop.

If you are going to buy an empty place with several rooms, do a feasibility study of how many treatment rooms you will be able to fit in and if you will be able to furnish them all and use them. Ideally, your salon should have:

☐ your treatment rooms

☐ reception area

☐ waiting room

☐ store room

☐ kitchen

☐ toilet and washroom

☐ staff room (if space allows).

Produce a business plan. In Chapters 1 and 8 we discuss the importance of having a good business plan and cash-flow forecast; follow the instructions and use them. It is no use opening a four treatment-room salon if you can afford to furnish and use only two of them.

Settling on a name and logo

The importance of a good name and an eye-catching logo is often underestimated. The first thing any potential customer comes across is the name of your business and your logo. Try to choose an appropriate name and a stylish logo to go with the name, as both of these are seen constantly. Your business name and logo will be used on your business cards, price lists, headed paper, compliment slips and shopfront as well as your website. Your clients will remember your salon by its name and will recognise and identify your business by the logo. Both of these will have an impact on your clientèle, especially through marketing and advertising.

The name you select must be easy to remember, a bit different if possible, relevant to your business and what you are offering, and must, of course, be appropriate.

For example 'Relaxing Hands Salon' would not be appropriate for a beauty salon, while 'Beauty 4 U' would be. The name is often what *you* would like your business to be called. It's like parents naming their baby – you choose what you like. Some people use their own name, some use the name of their town or street.

If you are artistic, you might want to design a logo yourself. It will give you a good feeling and cost you nothing. Alternatively, you can commission a graphic designer.

Although having a good name and logo is essential, try not to employ someone to give you advice or do the design unless you have a lot of spare money. Talk to your friends and family and get some of their ideas; there is always someone who can suggest and help you do it without incurring a lot of costs.

Buying, renting, or leasing

To find your new premises, you could start by looking in local or regional newspapers where business owners and commercial estate agents advertise. This is a good way of getting a 'feel' of the prices. Sometimes by driving or walking around the area of your choice you may find empty shops for sale. Otherwise, the best source is commercial estate agents; these are estate agents who deal only with businesses and shops.

Commercial estate agents are a good source of information and can help you find either an empty shop or a business for sale. They can do the negotiation and advise you on rents, rates and council matters, and liaise with your solicitor. You don't pay them anything: the seller pays their fee.

BUYING

You can buy a shop/premises outright. This is called buying the freehold where the land and the building become yours and you will become the owner of the property. This will involve very large sums of money, but is an excellent form of investment for the long term.

RENTING

If your financial resources are limited and you don't want to commit for the long term but are confident of growth, you can rent a premises with one, two or three rooms, for a fixed period with an option to renew your agreement. You will pay your rent either monthly or weekly. Your council tax will either be included or you will have to pay it yourself. However, you will be responsible for all other items such as gas, electricity, water and telephone. You will be expected to do your own decoration, and any modifications will require permission from the owner.

 Before signing any contract, make sure your solicitor checks it to ensure that all your legal rights are protected.

LEASING

The most common way of starting a salon in the High Street is to buy the lease of a shop. This means the land and property remain someone else's (called the landlord), but you become the owner of the shop (lease owner) for a fixed agreed period, say five or ten years, with certain terms and conditions and often restrictions. For this, you may or may not pay a lump sum of money (this is called a premium) but you will have to pay the council rates as well as a monthly or quarterly rent to the landlord. You will be responsible for all the repairs and maintenance and insurance of the premises you lease. During the term of the lease you can sell the lease and your business, or wait to the end of its term, negotiate and renew your lease, or you can just walk away.

If your finances allow, buying the lease of a place is the most common and exciting way of having your own business. When you decide to buy a leasehold shop, there are two options open to you. One is to buy an empty shop and turn it into your own dream beauty salon. The other is to buy an existing beauty business as a going concern.

Buying or renting empty premises

To buy or rent an empty place gives you the freedom to design it the way you want, with your own colour scheme, layout and features. You choose your furniture, products and equipment, and give the salon the name and logo that you like.

The pros and cons of empty premises
Pros

☐ You choose and create a new image for your beauty salon.

☐ You can start small and grow gradually.

☐ You may have to pay a small premium but sometimes nothing.

□ You should be able to negotiate more favourable terms.

□ It is far more exciting, and more of a challenge.

Cons

□ Landlord's and local council planning permission may be required for change of use.

□ A lot of hard work in refurbishment, design and possibly building work will be involved.

□ You will have to source and buy new furniture, equipment and products.

□ It will take time to build up the business, and back-up finance may well be needed.

□ Initially, it is more costly. It will involve professional fees from surveyors and lawyers to draw up plans and the lease. Invariably you will be asked to pay the landlord's legal costs as well.

 **Do your homework on the area, the size of the premises, and the terms and conditions of the lease, especially the rent and renewal. Get professional advice on this and make sure you negotiate not only the costs, but also the terms of your new lease.**

Taking on a lease on commercial premises is exciting, challenging and exhausting. Always get a good team of recommended professionals to advise you and help you through the process. Then listen to and act on their advice. Consult a qualified surveyor to make sure that the premises are structurally sound and do not require immediate major repairs to such things as the roof or drains. Your lawyer will tell you about your legal obligations under the lease for maintenance and repair of both your shop and the building, and whether it is your sole or a joint responsibility with other tenants.

Most landlords will require bank and personal references and a three- to six-month rent deposit. In addition, some also require that you give personal guarantees on the rent. Consider this carefully as, if your new business fails and you default on the rent, the landlord may sue you and go after your personal assets, as well as your home in the worst-case scenario.

Buying an existing business

To buy an ongoing beauty business is the other option. An existing business is often sold for one of two reasons. Either the owner (called the vendor) is retiring or has other personal reasons, or because the business is doing badly.

If you decide to buy an ongoing beauty business, you should find out exactly what you are buying and what you are getting for your money. Make sure the business is in the right location for you and is the right size for you to manage. There are a lot of factors involved, and unless you have had previous experience, you must employ an accountant to analyse the performance of the business for at least the past three years (turnover, profit/loss, margins, stock) using all the accounts and figures available (this is known as due diligence). Your solicitor will look into the legal side of the business, and the terms and conditions and the period of the lease.

 The use of a good accountant and an experienced solicitor in this field, and the advice they will give you, are vitally important if you decide to buy an existing beauty business.

You may buy the business with everything in it, including all the furniture, equipment, stock and even the staff. This is known as buying Lock, Stock and Barrel.

 You should find out everything about the business and the reason behind the sale before you agree to a purchase. It is very easy to get excited and carried away. Do your homework before investing your money.

THE PROS AND CONS OF AN EXISTING BUSINESS

Pros

☐ The business is already established, has a clientèle and is taking money.

□ You may not have to do any building work, decoration or refurbishment if the premises are in good order.

□ If it is an established beauty salon, your initial work will be much simpler.

□ It is easier to get a bank loan and get credit from existing suppliers.

Cons

□ You will most likely have to pay a lump sum as premium. This will depend on the remaining length of the lease, and the turnover and profit of the business.

□ You will have to live and work with someone else's choice of products and treatments for a time.

□ You will take on some staff who may not be to your liking and it could prove complicated to change the situation.

□ The business may have a tarnished reputation.

 **Don't be put off by a business which is not doing well and is up for sale. It is often because it is badly managed. If it is in the right location and at a knocked-down price, with good management and the right changes it can be made profitable (this is known as turning it around). This is the most exciting and challenging operation of any business and can be extremely profitable.**

Planning the design of your salon

The design and 'look' of the salon is often an expression of your taste and personality. It is very important to create a welcoming and relaxing atmosphere for clients. It is also very important that you decide on the type of salon you want to achieve: a relaxed spa, a city-centre salon offering quick treatments for time-short city workers, or a specialist beauty clinic. Try to keep to a theme or colour that runs throughout the salon to give a cohesive image to your enterprise. For example, our salon in London has mainly white walls, with black towels and black uniforms for the therapists, and cream for stationery to give a very clean and modern look. The shopfront is also black. Other themes to consider are natural materials (such as

25

coarse cottons or smooth silks) combined with beige or browns; Paris boudoir with velvets in rich colours and period furniture; or maybe a 'coffee shop' feel with comfy sofas and an informal look to the treatment rooms. Choose your colour or theme to run through all aspects of design, from the outside frontage, interior walls, flooring, uniforms, towels and couch covers to the treatment menu and all your printing and stationery. This will give your salon an 'image' or 'brand' with which your customers can associate.

 The style and colour scheme you choose should remain consistent throughout. Try to keep the décor simple: it is easier to maintain.

 Make sure your design and layout provide a comfortable and relaxing atmosphere – your clients expect this. You will get a lot of ideas for colour schemes, decoration and interior layouts, as well as display features, by visiting other salons. Exhibitions are another good source of inspiration.

There are many interior design and shop-fitting companies. Get two or three designs (normally free) and quotes, and if – and only if – your finances allow, choose one. Some beauty equipment supply companies offer a salon-planning service for a fee and will produce a suggested layout and give recommendations about various equipment as well.

Selecting your tradespeople

Doing internal building work and alterations, changing the use of a shop and remodelling an existing business premises will need professional builders and other tradespeople such as electricians, gas engineers and plumbers.

Recommendation is usually the best way of selecting your workforce or tradesmen. But even so, always make sure that they are reputable, fully qualified and registered with the right professional organisations. Then get at least three different companies or tradespeople to give you like-for-like quotes.

Compare these quotations and when you are deciding which one to choose, consider the following:

☐ How long the company or the builder has been in business.

☐ What guarantee you get.

☐ Evidence of their work.

☐ How well and clear their quotation is written.

☐ Whether they can give you any testimonials that you can verify.

 Make your final choice using all the above information and of course take into account the prices they have given you. Remember, the cheapest is not necessarily the best.

Planning the interior layout of your salon

If you are converting an empty shop, or one which was used for a different business, into a beauty salon, there are many things that have to be changed or incorporated into the new premises. Although your local council will inform you of all their regulations and requirements, and your various tradespeople will assist you with many of the things you have not thought of, it is advisable to have your own list.

THINGS TO BE CONSIDERED

☐ Various licences

☐ Planning permission

☐ Landlord's consent

☐ Heating

☐ Lighting

☐ Flooring

☐ Cooling system

- ☐ Plumbing

- ☐ Alarm

- ☐ CCTV

- ☐ Fire protection

- ☐ Laundry

- ☐ Storage

- ☐ Reception

- ☐ Telephone

- ☐ PDQ machine for taking credit card payments

- ☐ Internet connection

- ☐ Disabled access

- ☐ External signs

- ☐ Stationery

- ☐ Normal and hazardous waste disposal

- ☐ Furniture

- ☐ Treatment equipment

- ☐ Tools

- ☐ Accessories

- ☐ Towels

- ☐ Uniforms

- ☐ Treatment products

- ☐ Retail stock.

If your building work involves new partitioning walls and doors or if you are making a change of use to the premises (say from a boutique to a beauty salon), then the following must be considered:

☐ Permission must be obtained from the landlord *before* commencing any building works. A reputable builder will help you to navigate through the minefield of party wall and building regulations.

☐ Planning permission must be obtained from your local council for change of use *before* you buy the shop.

☐ Fire- and sound proofing of internal walls (if you are erecting new partitioning walls).

☐ Fire alarm system.

☐ Emergency lighting.

☐ Illuminated exit signs.

☐ Fire extinguishers (a must) and sprinklers (if necessary).

☐ Emergency exit.

☐ Facilities for the disabled.

☐ Heating system for cold weather.

☐ Cooling system for hot days.

☐ Hot and cold water in all treatment rooms.

☐ Plumbing for washing machine and tumble dryer.

☐ Adequate electrical sockets for all your equipment and electrical appliances, and some extra ones.

Your salon will need a good reception area, with a counter, a till and a telephone. Your treatment rooms should be of a size to house all the equipment and furniture that you need without them being cramped. Space allowing, you will also need a comfortable waiting room for the early arrivals where they can relax and enjoy a cup of herbal tea or a glass of water while reading a magazine. You will need a toilet and washing area with hand basin to be used by the customers as well as your staff.

You will also need a small kitchen area where tea and coffee can be made, staff can have their lunch and tea breaks, and where you could possibly put your washing machine and tumble dryer. Finally, a storage room is very useful for storing stock, cleaning materials and stationery.

CHOOSING FLOORING

Selecting your salon's flooring is an important decision. Good flooring can be expensive but it is necessary if it is to meet the demands of everyday commercial use.

The following points should be taken into account when you are deciding on flooring. Make sure:

☐ it is hard wearing

☐ it can be cleaned easily

☐ it is comfortable to stand and work on

☐ it has a non-slip surface

☐ it is not too noisy when people walk on it; some tiles look great but can be very noisy if walked on in heels

☐ it looks good and blends in with your salon's colour scheme.

THERAPY ROOMS

Therapy rooms should be of a reasonable size as you will need to be able to move around the couch freely and have easy access to your equipment. The walls should be painted with a satin or other washable paint for ease of cleaning. You could consider posters or pictures on the walls advertising new products and treatments, or photos with relaxing images. Tiles on the lower half of the walls or over the entire wall are very hard wearing, resilient to knocks, can easily be wiped clean and do not need painting. However, if laser or IPL (Intense Pulsed Light) is being performed in the room then it is important that these tiles are not shiny as light-reflective surfaces such as shiny tiles or mirrors are not allowed in the room for health and safety reasons.

The therapy room should have hot and cold water, a covered waste bin, plenty of electrical sockets, good ventilation, heating for winter and a cooling system for hot days. A dimmer switch for the light is better than an ordinary on-off switch as it allows you to vary the setting.

Disposal of hazardous waste is a very important issue and is taken seriously by local councils. A special 'sharps' container should be available in every therapy room and used for all electrolysis needles, micro-lancers and foot blades.

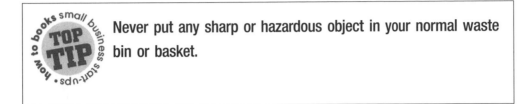

Never put any sharp or hazardous object in your normal waste bin or basket.

Displaying retail products in your therapy room encourages clients to look at, handle and buy them. Shelving can be used to display retail products, particularly if they are to support the treatments. But do bear in mind that these items may go missing if the room is left unattended. You may decide that a locked glass display cabinet is a more secure choice.

Remember that sales start in the treatment room and if a client can touch the product and ask questions while having a treatment it is much easier for the therapist to close a sale.

The best way to get the most from your therapy rooms is to make them multi-purpose, as opposed to designing each room for a specific purpose such as waxing or facials. This means that the rooms must be easily adaptable. Trolleys can be prepared for waxing or facials and be wheeled from room to room as needed.

The actual layout and design of your salon will depend on several factors but mainly on the existing walls. Some partitioning can produce different shapes and sizes. The layout of a typical treatment room is shown in Figure 2.1. The minimum recommended size of a treatment room is 3.2m × 2.5m.

RECEPTION

Whether your salon is on a prime High Street with a large reception area or has a shared reception at a hairdresser's or leisure centre, the potential client's first point of contact is reception and this is where the first impression of your business is made. It is for this reason that the reception is possibly the most important area of your salon. It should be welcoming, well lit and enticing while being the organisational hub of the salon.

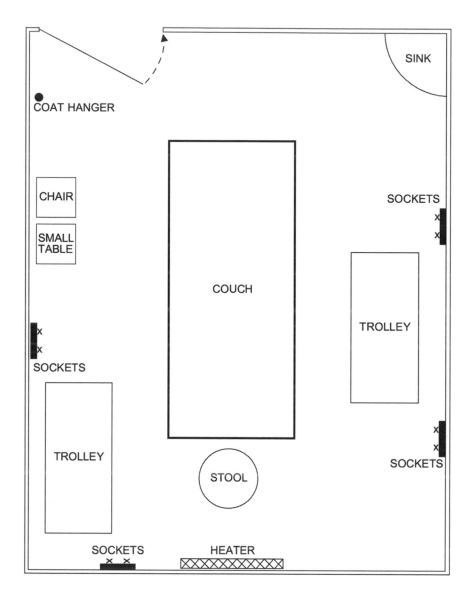

Figure 2.1 Layout of a typical treatment room

Your reception will have a counter, a till, telephone, PDQ machine, samples of your products and client information cards (if you are not computerised). Your business registration certificate, insurance certificates and special treatment licence should all be discreetly displayed.

The counter or front desk should be clean and tidy and uncluttered. It will have your appointment book and a telephone with an answering system so that you don't miss any calls from potential customers. The impression given should be of a calm, businesslike organisation. Hide all your bits and pieces such as pens and paper at a lower level out of view. The front desk leaves a lasting impression on any client and is often the place for impulse purchases.

WAITING ROOM

If you have sufficient space, you should incorporate a separate waiting room with comfortable seating, a coffee table and plenty of magazines and journals, all beauty-related of course. Make sure this room has good lighting, adequate heating for winter and is well cooled in the summer. Soft background music will make the place more relaxing and should always be played here. All your clients who are going to wait for their treatments should be offered a drink and told who will be seeing them and in approximately how long.

If your premises are limited in space, then the waiting area can be located in the reception.

 Make sure that there are enough electrical points for all the equipment needed at reception, such as the telephone, fax, computer, till and credit card terminal. This will be much safer and tidier than using extension leads.

STORE ROOM

Ideally the store room should be easily accessible to staff but not near client areas. A lockable door will ensure security is maintained. This room should contain shelving for the storage of products and be organised in a logical way for quick and easy retrieval of items. All consumables such as couch rolls, wax, manicure requisites, uniforms, towels and toiletries should be kept here. It is important that this area, as with all other areas of the salon, is always kept tidy and clean and is not damp.

 Using very basic shelving and cupboards for the store room will save you money. There is a variety of reasonably-priced storage shelving available from IKEA, Wickes or B&Q which can be assembled easily and within minutes.

KITCHEN AND UTILITY ROOM

A room where tea and coffee is made and your staff can have their tea and lunch breaks is extremely useful. At the same time you can put your washing machine and dryer in this room. You will obviously need ample electrical sockets and plumbing for your appliances. Needless to say, this room, like everywhere else, must always be tidy and clean, not only for hygiene purposes but also in case your clients happen to see it. If your finances allow, a small fridge freezer and a microwave will also be very useful for staff use as well as occasional customer requirements.

RETAIL AREA

Every beauty salon must have retail products for sale. The reason for this is twofold:

1. The use of retail products on the back of treatment is what the beauty industry is all about. A lot of products have been developed to be used in conjunction with and in between treatments at home, while some others are made purely for the client's use after consultation with a beautician.

2. The sale of retail products will generate extra income and boosts the cash flow of the business.

To achieve a good turnover from the sale of products you should allocate a suitable area to display and promote them. These are generally displayed in the reception area of the salon where it is convenient for members of the public to have a browse. When designing and arranging your retail area the following points should be taken into account:

☐ Use attractive shelving and display units.

☐ Make sure the products are well lit and comfortably accessible.

☐ Display the best-selling lines at eye level.

☐ Put your very expensive products in locked cabinets.

☐ Always have someone to advise and assist the customer.

☐ Make sure there are testers and samples for people to try. Most of your suppliers will provide testers and samples; some will even supply a special stand for this purpose.

☐ Ensure that all your products are clearly priced and are not out of date.

□ Make sure that your receptionist and all of your staff are well trained about these products and have some selling skills.

□ Offer sales incentives to your staff in the form of commission. This will encourage them to sell products and boost your revenue.

The display of retail beauty products should not be limited to the retail area. It is a good idea to display some of them in the treatment rooms, allowing the therapists to show them to clients.

 If possible, you should have at least one full-time member of staff looking after your retail area. The income generated from selling products can be quite substantial if the person is a good salesperson.

Obtaining a Special Treatment Licence

Some local councils require a Premises Special Treatment Licence. You will have to apply for this licence and after a visit and inspection by officials from your council, a certificate will be issued outlining what treatment you are licensed to carry out and what you cannot do. They may also specify other requirements with regard to the size of your treatment rooms, installation of hot and cold water and hygiene and safety with which you must comply.

Access to a sink with hot and cold water is very important for hygiene and treatment purposes, even if it is not required by your local council.

 Council officials will from time to time visit your salon unexpectedly to carry out an inspection. Always comply with their requirements and be prepared.

Installing sound proofing

Sound proofing the treatment room should also be seriously considered, both from a relaxation viewpoint as well as confidentiality for the client. All reputable builders and carpenters are familiar with the regulations regarding sound proofing and should automatically sound proof as well as fire proof all new partitioning walls and doors.

It doesn't instil confidence in the client in the waiting room if they can hear screams of waxing pain, or the details of last night's date, from the treatment room.

Playing music in the salon

Beauty salons and spas are often associated with being places of relaxation. Treatments such as facial or massage or even manicure/pedicure should be complemented by soft relaxing background music. Most salons choose a selection of classical music for this purpose. One way of providing music is to have a centralised system wired up to all rooms, including the waiting room and reception. Another simpler way is to have individual CD players or iPods/MP3s in each room. Soft music creates a calm atmosphere and puts your clients in a relaxed mood. It is also believed that music improves the therapist's performance. However, remember that if you play music in a public place or to members of the public you will by law need two licences:

1. The first one is called PPL (Phonographic Performance Ltd). This is an organisation which looks after the copyright in public performance of the sound recordings. It collects licence fees from anyone who broadcasts music to members of the public and passes them to the record companies and the performers that they represent. To apply for a licence or to get more information, you can contact the company through www.ppluk.com or by calling them on 0207 534 1000.

2. The second organisation is called PRS (Performing Rights Society). The licence fee collected by this company is for the benefit of the writers and publishers of the music. This company's telephone number is 0800 068 4828 and the website is www.prsformusic.com

Using flowers and candles

Scented candles (health and safety regulations permitting) and fresh flowers are also very common to spas and beauty salons as not only do they give the salon a welcoming feel, they also make the salon look and feel calm and relaxing.

Putting together a window display

If you have selected your shop with a glass frontage (shop window), then not only will your salon benefit from good natural light, it will also attract people into the salon and enable you to have an attractive display of your products and treatments.

Your window is your advertisement for your salon, so make sure you project the best image possible. Here are some points to consider:

1. Keep it simple; uncluttered and uncomplicated displays are the most effective.

2. Make your window stand out from the rest with a bold colour or design.

3. Check that you have the balance right by stepping back and looking at your window from outside your salon.

4. Change the display at least once a month to keep interest.

5. Do seasonal treatment and product promotions. For example, spray tan and sun products in the summer, and a Halloween theme or Christmas decorations with appropriate products.

6. Be professional in your presentation by avoiding handwritten signs or blutac. It is not expensive to have signs printed and you can store them in an art folder to be used again.

7. Use posters and pictures that your product suppliers send you.

8. Make sure that your exterior and interior windows are regularly cleaned and that the shelving is dust-free.

Installing a security alarm

An alarm system is another useful thing to consider, especially when in a lot of cases it is a basic requirement by insurance companies. Although initially it could be expensive to set up, it reduces your insurance premiums and is good for your own peace of mind. When choosing your alarm company, make sure that your system is covered 24 hours a day for emergencies and that the system goes through to the local police station. There are many companies that provide this service, including www.adt.co.uk, www.gardsec.co.uk and www.homeguardsecurity.co.uk

Ensuring salon safety

One area that you cannot afford to neglect is the safety features within your salon. Although most of the essential features are compulsory by law, your local council and the insurance companies will insist on them. Installation of fire alarms, sprinkler or fire extinguisher systems, special fire doors, emergency lighting and emergency exits are not luxuries but essentials for the safety of your clients, your staff and yourself.

☐ Installation of your fire alarm system and emergency lighting will be done by your electrician.

☐ Fire protection and sprinkler or fire extinguisher system is provided by many independent companies with yearly service contracts. You could try www.cityfire.co.uk or www.chubb.co.uk

☐ Special fire-check or fire-resisting doors, and emergency exits will be installed by your builder.

Disposing of toxic and hazardous waste

Naturally your salon will have waste and rubbish to be disposed of. Your normal waste is classified as commercial waste and is collected by the council for a fee. Some councils sell you special black or grey bags and you can use only these.

Your toxic or hazardous waste which could potentially be harmful or dangerous must not be put in your normal rubbish bags, as the council will not take them. There are specialist companies which will come, say, once a month or every three months and take the toxic and hazardous waste away for a fee. For example, razor blades and needles must be stored in a safe metal box and put away immediately, until they are collected. We will discuss this subject again in Chapter 3.

Installing electricity and gas

With regard to your electricity and gas, don't cut corners and don't compromise. Have both of these checked for safety. You should consider the electrical wiring of the premises and whether this needs to be updated to meet electrical standards as required by Electricity at Work Regulations BS 7671. You will also need to consider the room layouts so that the sockets can be put in the correct places for ease of use. A good electrician will help you with these matters when you discuss the location of your equipment and furniture. Any gas work must be carried out only by someone who is on the Gas Safe Register. Any plumber or gas engineer who installs or services gas-related equipment or appliances must by law be qualified and registered and hold a certificate from this organisation.

 When the electricity or gas work is completed you should receive a safety certificate. Your electrician should give you an electrical safety certificate, and your gas engineer will give you a gas safety certificate which is issued by the Gas Safe Register.

You may find that your local council requires that all the electrical equipment is inspected and given a safety certificate at regular intervals (either yearly or every three or five years). There are specialist companies that will do this for you.

Heating the salon

The purpose of a beauty treatment is to make the client feel comfortable, warm and relaxed. Maintaining the temperature of the salon at a comfortable level for both clients and staff is imperative. When designing and refurbishing your salon, ensure that all the rooms have adequate heating for winter and proper ventilation and a cooling system for hot, stuffy days. What constitutes a comfortable temperature depends on what you are doing. According to The Workplace (Health, Safety and Welfare) Regulations 1992, the temperature at a place of work should be 16°C within the first hour of the start of a day's work. However, for a client who is semi-dressed, the therapy rooms themselves would need to be at a much higher temperature of around 22°C to be comfortable.

The salon can be heated by either gas or electric central heating using radiators, or by electric convection heaters or electric storage heaters which use low-cost, off-peak electricity.

 Discuss and take advice from your builder and electrician regarding the type of heating you should install. This will greatly depend on the size and layout of your premises. Make sure you take into account the installation and running costs.

Ventilating the salon

Your salon also needs good ventilation and a cooling system. Efficient ventilation is necessary to prevent too much moisture in the air causing condensation and an unpleasant stuffy atmosphere. A good ventilation system must change the air several times an hour while not causing draughts. At its most basic level this could be a window. However, the arrangement of your salon, access to fresh air, the type of ceilings you have and your finances will ultimately decide whether or not you can install an air-conditioning system.

Lighting the salon

The lighting in a salon should be flexible and adaptable to suit the variety of situations you will encounter in a normal working day. You will probably have to install different types in different locations. For example, your toilet will have a simple single light, while your retail area will need attractive spotlights and possibly cabinet lighting.

The lighting in the therapy rooms needs to be able to change from dimmed and mellow during a massage or facial, to bright while the therapist is doing intense detailed work such as eyelash tinting or extractions. Localised lighting on a stand is portable, efficient and can be turned off when not required. Overhead lighting should ideally be on a dimmer to vary the intensity of light and to alter the mood and ambience of the room. Magnifying glasses with lamps are an essential in every treatment room where precise, close work is done.

Purchasing the basics

For your basic essentials, join wholesale outlets such as Makro or Costco where you can buy towels, cleaning materials, toilet rolls, tea and coffee at wholesale prices. You will need to prove that you are either self employed or a bona-fide business. They normally need a business card or your company's headed paper with name and address, and an identity card from you.

Also, shops such as IKEA and Homebase offer excellent value for money for items such as glasses, mirrors, bowls, baskets, etc.

 Remember that controlling costs and spending is very important and will pay dividends. Most businesses fail, not through lack of customers, but because they failed to control costs.

3
SALON MANAGEMENT

IN THIS CHAPTER

- ☐ How to be a good salon manager

- ☐ Keeping the salon clean

- ☐ Employing the right staff

- ☐ Reception – the most important part of the salon

- ☐ Stock control

- ☐ Dealing with injuries and emergencies

- ☐ Securing your salon.

To run your salon efficiently and professionally you will need to have a structured programme and be a good manager. As a manager there are things that you have to understand, do and recognise. There are certain jobs and tasks that should be done daily, others that need to be sorted out on a weekly basis and some that need to be done only once a month. Some tasks you can give to others to do and you only supervise. There must be rules and regulations, policies and procedures that must be followed by everyone. Apart from the normal treatments which everyone has to do (and that includes the majority of owners who try to manage their salon as well as doing treatments), the salon will run smoothly only if everyone knows their role, what they are meant to do and when they should do it.

The manager's role

Business management is analysed and dealt with in Chapter 8. Here we look at the day-to-day running of the salon and managing the salon, staff and customers.

Although it is not recommended, if you decide to do treatments as well as manage your salon, you will need to fully understand certain issues which will enable you to carry out both jobs at the same time. Here are some of them:

1. Set aside time for each job: treatment time and managing time. Stick to this timetable.

2. You must understand the daily needs of your salon.

3. You have to understand your staff and know how to deal with their individual characters.

4. You should encourage good communication with and among staff members.

5. Meet the needs of your customers, who are ultimately your 'paymasters' (the lifeblood of your business).

6. Always be fully aware of what is going on in the salon.

7. Avoid chaos and ensure the smooth running of the salon by having systems in place that help everyone to do their jobs properly, and in line with your salon's rules, policies and procedures.

8. Delegate responsibility for various tasks and make sure they are done correctly.

9. Make everyone accountable for their actions and behaviour.

10. Lead your staff by example; do everything the way you expect your staff to do it.

11. Do not try to control your staff.

12. Always be calm and relaxed, even when everything is hectic.

Providing an efficient and friendly service

The first point of contact with your salon for all of your clients will be the reception, be it by phone or by walking in. Answering the client politely and correctly is essential for that positive first impression. The following points add to the efficiency of your salon and should be followed:

☐ Every customer should be greeted with a smile and offered help or assistance. For example, the receptionist can say, 'Good morning, my name is Tina, can I help you?'

☐ If the client has come for a booking, then they should be asked if this is their first visit, what the appointment is for and the desired time. The booking must be made correctly, taking full details of the customer, and giving the customer an appointment card with details of the appointment on it.

□ If the customer is in for advice or for a product, ensure that full attention is given to them. Listen carefully to what they say and reply accordingly. Whatever you do, make sure that the customer leaves the salon satisfied and happy.

□ When a customer phones the salon, it is important that a clear and friendly voice replies and that the call does not go straight to answerphone.

□ A typical phone greeting could be, 'Thank you for calling Beauty 4U, Claire speaking. How can I help you?'

□ Whenever possible, ensure that your therapists do not run late. If this happens, explain to the visiting client the reason and length of the delay and pleasantly apologise. Lead the client to the waiting room and offer them a drink and some reading materials.

□ If possible, discreetly inform the therapist that their next client has arrived.

□ After a while, go to see the waiting client and make sure everything is OK. If possible, inform them of how much longer they may have to wait.

□ Never discuss any problem and never argue with or tell a therapist off in front of clients.

□ Always make sure that your booking system is in proper order, so that there is no confusion about the therapists, time or nature of treatment when appointments are made.

□ Samples, price lists, information packs, pens, etc. should always be in their right places and everyone should know where everything is.

□ Before a treatment commences, therapists should ensure that everything is ready. This will prevent the customer having to wait while your staff desperately look everywhere for something they need.

□ Details of every customer and the date and type of treatments must be recorded on a client record card. Any health issue or other relevant information must be filled in. This can be done on a computer if you use one for your records.

☐ Finally, every customer expects a friendly and efficient service; make sure you give it to them, or they will not come back.

We will discuss most of these points in more detail later in the book.

Maintaining hygiene and cleanliness

Maintaining a very high standard of hygiene and cleanliness is vital to your salon. This is something which should be practised by all personnel from day one and maintained every day. Hygiene and cleanliness is not something just for the treatment rooms, couches and equipment. It should run through every part of the salon, including the staff room, toilet, the sink, under the sink and everything else that does not move. It also applies to the therapists, beauticians and other members of staff. It is vital to prevent cross-infection and to safeguard the interest of both the clients and the therapists. Here are some useful suggestions:

☐ The treatment rooms, including the wax pots, should be cleaned spotless *after every client*.

☐ New couch covers and towels must be used for *every client*.

☐ Whenever reusable tools are used, they must be sterilised thoroughly after *every treatment*.

☐ New waxing spatulas must be used for *each client*.

☐ Uniforms should be clean, washed and unsoiled *at all times*.

☐ All trolleys and work surfaces should be wiped with *disinfectant daily*.

☐ Make sure that all members of staff know what they need to do to keep the salon clean and safe.

☐ Display a list of cleaning tasks that must be done on a daily, weekly and monthly basis.

☐ Organise a deep clean of the salon if it is quiet.

☐ Sterilising and sanitising rules and procedures should be clearly displayed near the sinks, both in the treatment rooms and in the manicure area, with all the necessary equipment and products clearly marked and available for use.

It is essential to prevent cross-infection, either between client and therapist, or client and client, by cleaning, disinfecting and sterilising all equipment and tools. It is important for the salon owner and manager to recognise the differences between these procedures.

 Immaculate standards of hygiene will influence a client's choice of salon in these days of increased awareness of infection. All members of staff must be well-groomed with clean hair and nails and subtle make-up; they are the walking advert for your business.

Cleaning should be done routinely to remove dust, grease, hair or dirt from the salon, its equipment and tools. The salon should be swept, the floor washed and dust removed from all surfaces and rooms on a daily basis.

Disinfection reduces the number of micro-organisms to a level low enough to make infection unlikely. It is usually carried out using chemicals such as Barbicide or diluted bleach or other disinfectants.

Sterilisation is the process of making items sterile. With the increased spread and awareness of HIV, hepatitis C and funguses, it is vital to safeguard ourselves, our clients and our business by ensuring the sterilising of all tools. All implements that are required to be sterile must be cleaned in hot water and soap, then dried and finally sterilised using your chosen method. There are four main methods of sterilisation in the beauty salon.

1. Chemicals. There are several brands on the market, the best known being Barbicide. They can be decanted into spray bottles which are kept at every sink and manicure or pedicure station, to be sprayed on clean tools immediately prior to treatment, thereby reassuring the client.

2. UV cabinet. After cleaning, your tools, sponges and files can be stored in a UV (ultra-violet) cabinet to inhibit the growth of bacteria. However, the items must be clean prior to being put in the cabinet as UV light has limited penetration and any oil or debris renders it ineffective.

3. Glass-bead steriliser. Tiny glass beads contained in a protective case are heated to a temperature of $190°$ to $300°C$. It is compact, easy to use and quick, sterilising small metal implements such as manicure tools and tweezers in five minutes.

4. Autoclave. This is a closed unit that increases the temperature of boiling water to 110° to 135°C, destroying all bacterial and fungal spores. This is by far the most effective and efficient method for sterilising metal tools.

Disposing of waste

Give careful consideration to the disposal of your waste, including hazardous materials, and recycle where possible. The following is a list of suggested guidelines:

☐ Rubbish bins should be conveniently placed in every treatment room. They should have disposable liners and be kept free from old wax or other products.

☐ Bins should be emptied every day, or before they are full, and placed inside a larger rubbish bag which should be put outside in the street for collection according to your council's commercial waste procedures. In Westminster in central London, all commercial waste must be put in specially-bought grey commercial waste bin bags and placed outside only between 7a.m. and 10a.m. Failure to comply could lead to a £1000 fine, so check your local council rules.

☐ Recycle where possible. Cardboard boxes should be flattened and taken to the recycling point, along with plastic and glass containers and paper, unless of course your council collects them.

☐ Hazardous waste will need special care and a different arrangement has to be made for its disposal. Your local council will again be able to offer advice and guidance on this. The most common hazards in the beauty salon are blades, needles and other sharp disposable items which must be disposed of in a special sharps container.

☐ The *sharps container* should be easily recognisable, durable, puncture-proof and lockable. Take your sharps box to your local hospital for incineration when full.

☐ If you do generate toxic waste, again talk to your council for advice. In a lot of cases a specialist company will have to come to your salon and remove this, for a fee.

 Never put toxic or hazardous waste in normal rubbish bags. It is dangerous and is an offence.

Organising laundry

Salons create a lot of washing, with towels, couch covers and uniforms needing daily washing and drying. Recently it has become popular to carry out face and body treatments using hot towels which are normally kept in a heated cabinet. This has increased the necessity for the daily washing of even more towels.

The most cost-effective method is to buy a good commercial washing machine and a tumble dryer for staff to operate throughout the day. There is an initial outlay for the machines, together with the continuous running costs of washing powder and electricity. But in the long run this will work out much cheaper than a laundry service. However, using a laundry service or service wash can save you time and provides a higher quality finish.

 Your staff uniforms should be of good-quality, non-iron material, so that they will last longer even when washed regularly, and are easier to look after.

Getting the first impression right

The first impression is the lasting impression. The first visit, the first phone call, the first advice; these are all either the beginning or the end of a client, depending on how they are treated, spoken to or advised and what impression they get from their experience. We have already discussed various aspects of this in Chapter 2. Here we look again at two important issues.

Employing professional, trained and informed staff

Having trained, knowledgeable and professional staff is essential if you are going to run a successful salon. One of the many reasons why clients seek help and advice from a beauty salon is for the specialist knowledge, training and experience that the therapists have. Draw on this knowledge and innate confidence that the client has in you by offering free consultations. You and your staff should be able to suggest the best course of treatment or products for the client to see effective results. Each client should be approached with a pleasant, caring and professional attitude, without the 'hard sell', to ensure trust and repeat visits. Clients pay for your time – they should get your undivided attention.

Ensure your staff are familiar with all the products you sell, the treatments you offer and your prices. If they don't have this information, the customer will lose confidence.

Managing the reception

Apart from the clean and welcoming look of the reception, what impresses clients and potential customers most is being able to speak to a pleasant receptionist when visiting or calling the salon. The receptionist needs to be well-informed on all aspects of products and treatments, and be able to give advice to the client on their beauty concerns. The receptionist should speak clearly and be able to make the right appointment for the customer.

 Spend time on finding the right person to run your reception. Remember the role of receptionist is the most important one in the salon. Not only does it improve the efficiency of your salon, it helps your business grow.

Many small beauty salons which run their businesses on very small budgets cannot afford a full-time receptionist. As a result, the majority of telephone calls go straight to the answerphone and sometimes are not replied to for several hours. Also, while all the therapists are in the treatment rooms, the door to the salon will be closed, with a hand-written note saying, 'Please ring the bell' or 'In treatment, back in half an hour'. Although there will be times when this is unavoidable, neither of these scenarios promotes a professional image and will not give a potential customer much confidence. Also, while the door is shut, any customer wanting to make an appointment or buy products may just walk away to another salon, resulting in a lost sale or client.

THE RECEPTIONIST'S DUTIES

Every salon operates slightly differently. But the general duties of your receptionist should include:

☐ Answering the phone.

☐ Greeting and welcoming clients.

☐ Booking appointments.

☐ Taking credit card and cash payments.

☐ Advising on and selling products.

☐ Cleaning the reception area, including floors and shelves.

☐ Changing the window and product displays (if you don't have a window dresser).

☐ Liaising with therapists about their clients and appointments.

☐ Ensuring the smooth running of the salon.

TAKING PAYMENTS

At reception you will need facilities to take payments with a till and a credit card machine (PDQ). Having the ability to take credit and debit cards is essential, as the majority of payments for services and products are made this way. Accepting cards opens up many more new sales opportunities, such as mail order, internet and payments over the phone, as well as encouraging impulse and larger spending.

Each time you take a card payment you will need authorisation from the card company. This is done through your PDQ machine, which is linked via a telephone line. It is important to have a separate telephone line and power supply so that the machine can operate independently. This will leave your salon's main telephone line free for incoming calls and will prevent paying customers having to wait to pay if the salon's phone line is busy with an incoming call.

There are several companies who will rent you the PDQ machine when you set up a merchant account for a monthly fee ranging from £5 for a static unit to £20 per month for a portable wireless model.

Banks will charge a fee for each transaction, which is usually a percentage of the transaction amount with credit cards (1% to 4% typically) or a flat fee for debit cards (e.g. 60p).

At the end of the day, through a simple process (details will be supplied to you by the PDQ machine company) your card transactions will be added and summarised for you. This process is called '*banking*'. The total figure from this must match that of your till for your cards transactions.

Most trade associations offer discounted rates for a credit card facility machine and preferential rates for transaction fees. It is worth contacting them and becoming a member.

Payments made by cheque should be avoided if possible as they are more liable to fraud. If you are presented with a cheque, particularly from an unknown client, always make sure:

☐ It has been filled out correctly and signed in front of you.

☐ It is presented with a cheque guarantee card.

☐ The signature on the cheque matches that on the cheque guarantee card.

☐ The cheque guarantee card is still valid. Then record the card number, sort code and date on the back of the cheque.

☐ The value of the cheque does not exceed the amount on the guarantee card, usually £50 to £100.

☐ Never to accept more than one cheque in any one day from the same customer where the total value of the cheques exceeds that of the cheque guarantee card.

As part of your accounts system, you will need to keep a record of all payments taken each day and what products have been sold, either by keeping a Daily Takings Book (also called Daily Sales Book) or with a till – preferably both. All your cash and cards received should be put into the till. It is good practice to ensure that all staff are trained in the use of the till and the PDQ machine. The receptionist and manager should also be aware of what to do if the machine breaks down, if authorisation is required or if fraud is suspected.

Make sure that there is a float in the till made up of sufficient change for the day, usually 20 £1 coins, two £5 and two £10 notes, depending on the needs of your business.

The Daily Takings Book is a great way to keep a record of treatments done and sales of products. It can simplify calculating commission payments to staff and also as proof of sale if a product is returned or in case of a complaint. The information that needs to be recorded is client name (if possible), method of payment (cash or card), total amount, treatment carried out and the product sold. If you use a computerised till system, all these will be done for you by the computer automatically.

 It is a requirement of HM Revenue and Customs that you keep all your financial records for six years. Make sure you do.

REFUNDS

The process of giving refunds is susceptible to fraud by employees and customers. It is worth having a system in place to minimise this possibility. The following is a list of suggestions:

☐ Only one or two persons, preferably a manager, should be authorised to give refunds.

☐ Ask and make a note of the reason why the product is being returned or a refund asked for.

☐ Make sure the item was purchased from you. Proof of purchase or receipt should be asked for and presented by the customer. Alternatively, check your Daily Takings Book to see when the customer bought the product and how they paid.

☐ The product should be in its original and unused packaging, unless it has been used and has caused a problem, in which case it is a complaint and needs to be investigated.

☐ All refunds should only be made in the same form that payment was taken. So if the customer paid with cash then cash should be given back. If a card was used then the same card is needed to refund the purchase.

☐ You must have a time limit for refunds (this varies, but is usually 30 days). This must be your company's policy and be clearly stated on your receipts, or explained to your customers verbally when a sale is made.

☐ Some suppliers will accept returns and will credit your account if the item is faulty or causes an allergic reaction.

BOOKING APPOINTMENTS

Taking phone calls and greeting customers to make appointments is another important role of the receptionist. Naturally your receptionist should be familiar with all aspects of treatments, how long each one takes, prices and special promotional offers. If you are using a computerised system, full training must be given before the receptionist is expected to be left alone to take bookings. If you are using a handwritten manual system, everything must be written clearly so that others can easily read and follow.

Whether you choose to write your appointments in a book or invest in a computerised system will depend largely on your finances. Computers can be expensive and complex to start with but in the long run they make life easier and smoother. The initial cost and the thought of learning a lot of complex computer operations often puts people off. However, once you have a system and use it, you will wonder how you ever worked without one.

If you decide to invest in one of these systems, see demonstrations from several companies and ask to talk to other salons that are using their system. Then compare the following:

☐ Ease of operation.

☐ Training.

☐ Support and 24-hour maintenance of the system.

☐ Adaptability and compatibility of the system to the requirements of your business.

☐ The cost.

 Make sure you are fully satisfied with all the above before signing the agreement and parting with your money, as it is a big investment.

Once the software has been installed and the operation learned, all your appointments, customers' details, daily sales, products sold and products in stock, ordering of products and many other bits of information can be monitored and obtained at the touch of a button.

Software systems are available that are linked to the till and have the added option of sending text messages reminding clients of their appointments, which is great for keeping no-shows to a minimum.

Another very useful feature of computerised systems is their use in stock control, which is discussed later. The long-established method of writing appointments into an appointment system in pencil is still the most popular with the majority of smaller salons, mainly because it is quick, easy to learn and economical.

Some customers prefer e-mailing for appointments. This is fine as long as you regularly check the e-mails. One major problem with this is the fact that it often involves several messages going backwards and forwards before an appointment is finalised.

A skilled receptionist can turn a simple treatment booking into a much more profitable appointment by:

☐ Suggesting services such as eyebrow shaping or back and neck massage as add-ons to leg waxing or facials.

☐ Offering the salon's special offers and promotions.

☐ Up-selling the treatment or selling a course of treatments.

☐ Offering follow-up appointments when a treatment is completed.

☐ Suggesting products.

☐ Receiving feedback from the client regarding their treatment and experience.

As impulse buys and decisions are often made at the reception desk, it very important that the staff are fully trained in product and treatment knowledge, so that they can advise the client with confidence.

The following list outlines some important points in the management of the reception:

☐ Standardise your telephone greeting. For example, 'Good morning Beauty 4U. Amanda speaking. How may I help?' This will reinforce a consistent image to callers.

☐ Answer all telephone calls promptly and return telephone messages within half an hour or less.

☐ All staff should know how long each treatment takes and which therapists are best trained for each treatment.

☐ Details needed for each appointment should include full name of the client, telephone number and treatment required. It is good practice to repeat back to the client these details to ensure they are correct.

☐ Allow sufficient time for every treatment.

☐ Mistakes will be avoided by asking details of the requested appointment. A common mistake is for the client to book a Bikini wax and actually want a Brazilian, which takes twice the time. On a busy day with appointments back-to-back this would mean either running late or a disappointed customer.

☐ Clients must be made aware of any cancellation policy that you have, such as a penalty for failure to give 24 hours' notice of cancellation.

☐ No-shows are a continual annoyance but a record must be kept to get to know the persistent offenders.

☐ All major treatments and appointments over one hour should be booked with details of a credit card taken from the client. These details must be securely recorded to avoid credit card fraud and to be in compliance with your obligations under the Data Protection Act.

☐ Back-to-back booking, discussed in Chapter 6, should be used wherever possible.

Booking appointments is also discussed in Chapter 6.

RETAIL SALES

If space allows, a dedicated area for retail products is a must in your salon. If you are extremely short of space, your treatment rooms and possibly waiting room should be utilised for the display of products relevant to your treatments.

Products should be attractively displayed on shelves and cabinets, clearly marked with the price. Make sure that shelves are dusted and cleaned every day and that the displays are changed regularly. Remember that purchasing products is often an emotional decision and your customer is more likely to buy if they can see, feel and touch the products. Unless they are very expensive items, don't keep products away in locked cupboards or behind the front desk – let your customer try out the product first, using a tester unit, and browse the shelves without feeling pressured. Of course, the receptionist or a therapist must be available to give advice and help if necessary.

The following list of suggestions will help you get the best from your retail products:

☐ Have a dedicated space for each brand, which is logically displayed either by product type (cleansers, moisturisers, etc.) or by skin type (oily, dry, anti-aging, etc.).

☐ Don't have too few or too many products on the shelves. The ideal stock level is three to six.

☐ Keep it simple. Product displays have more visual impact if they are uncluttered and simply and attractively displayed. Don't let your products be overshadowed.

☐ Keep products and shelves spotlessly clean and dust-free. Would you buy a product that was covered in a layer of dust?

☐ Good lighting is important to showcase your products and make them attractive to the passing visitor. Natural light gives a true reflection of colour, which is essential if you are retailing make-up, while spotlights can highlight and accentuate individual items.

☐ Eye level is buy level. This classic rule of merchandising is so true – always put the products that you want to promote on shelves that are at eye level with the customer.

☐ Focus attention on an individual product by promoting it in a prominent position where it can be easily seen. Accentuate the item by spotlighting.

☐ Regularly change the layout and display of your retail products to stimulate interest.

Do seasonal promotions linking products and treatments. For example, for a Valentine's Day promotion you could:

□ Create a colourful window display with red hearts.

□ Have helium-filled red heart balloons attached to your board outside the salon (if you have one).

□ Promote Brazilian hot waxing treatments.

□ Offer an unusual or different treatment to make your salon stand out from the rest. Consider pubic hair coloring or shapes such as a heart or even bikini gems.

□ Retail-related Valentine products such as Betty colour, heart-shaped jewellery or gift vouchers.

□ Offer nail art with a heart theme.

SEASONAL SALES IDEAS

Other seasonal promotions could include:

□ *Mother's/Father's Day.* Promote your gift vouchers as an ideal gift, or offer two treatments at the same time for a reduced price for mother and daughter pampering.

□ *Christmas.* Busiest time of the year!

□ *New Year.* January can be a quiet month, but try offering 10% off all treatments, including courses, in January and see how much busier this makes your business. This is the ideal time to offer courses or packages of treatments such as facials or slimming treatments, as customers often make a New Year's resolution to finally tackle their problems, such as weight gain or bad skin.

□ *Easter.* Good opportunity to offer chocolate-related treatments and products.

□ *American Independence Day.* Fun to offer American red, white and blue nail art.

Various sales and marketing ideas are also covered in Chapter 10.

TESTER UNIT

Some suppliers provide individual testers for each product. A few others supply (sometimes you have to pay for it) a complete tester unit with your opening order package. This should not be an optional extra; without it you will face a much harder challenge making a sale.

Testers are vital to your retail sales. Customers need to smell and touch the product, and often sample it. Whichever skincare or make-up company you choose, make sure you get as many testers and samples as possible. Remember to keep the testers clean and dust-free and ensure a good supply of tissues and cotton buds. It is important to provide product information and brochures, as these will enable your client to make an informed choice.

Dermalogica, probably one of the best known skincare brand in the world, is at the forefront of innovative retail merchandising and offers a formula that everyone can learn from. They supply a very attractive and compact tester unit which has proved invaluable. The secret of the company's success can mainly be attributed to their excellent and continuous training programme in both treatments and products. They offer full training of their products, treatments and retail sales free of charge. This gives a therapist who has been on their training course confidence and an excellent start in using and selling their range of treatments and products.

The company has also pioneered the concept of 'skin bar', followed by what they have called a 'Micro-Zone' which encourages clients to learn about products in an informal relaxed way. These are 20 to 30 minute zone specific treatments which offer on-the-spot solutions to the client's skin problems. The client doesn't have to pre-book or invest much time or money in solving their skincare concerns, answering today's need for quick solutions in clients' busy lives.

Giving samples can be a great way to allow a hesitant client to try before buying, but you should always allow the client the opportunity to purchase the product before doling out the sample. Make sure your samples are well marked and kept in an orderly manner so that the right sample can easily be found without having to search when you are busy.

Be selective in your sampling – give the client an opportunity to buy first. Limit the number of samples to three at one time. Make a note of the samples given on the customer's record card and follow up at the next visit.

Don't lose a sale. If your client wishes to make a purchase but you do not have the product in stock, write down what they need and their details in a client order book. This can be kept at reception and the client can be phoned when the item comes in. To maintain client loyalty and exceptional customer service, you can post the product at no extra charge. Although this shows excellent customer service, it is best to ensure that you always have enough stock in your salon to avoid this happening, as not everyone can wait for their product.

Controlling stock

If you are running a beauty salon it is important to understand and have systems in place in order to manage your stock, including both professional and retail products. You will need to know how much you have in stock at any one time so that you know what and when to reorder.

The benefits of an efficient stock-control system are:

□ Never running out of products.

□ Not over-stocking so your money isn't tied up in excess stock.

□ Product theft is spotted and deterred at an early stage.

Counting stock manually (stock taking) is best done by two people simultaneously to avoid mistakes. Alternatively, if you don't have a substantial amount, one person should do it then another check it to ensure accuracy. The preferred choices will be the salon owner and one other person; or the manager and one other person.

Generally speaking, the people who do the stock take should also be responsible for the following tasks:

□ Carrying out regular stock takes.

□ Maintaining records of deliveries, sales and damaged products.

□ Setting stock levels according to the popularity of the product.

☐ Reordering to maintain minimum and maximum stock levels.

☐ Keeping checks on sell-by dates of products.

☐ Stock rotation.

Stock taking should be done on a regular basis depending on the needs and turnover of your salon; weekly, fortnightly or monthly are the most common.

Manual stock control is keeping track of products by writing down each item on a spreadsheet. The products are first divided into suppliers, then further divided into product type, such as cleansers, moisturisers, etc., then size or colour, etc. This will make the task of completing the stock take quicker and easier if you can group similar items together. Some suppliers will provide you with pre-printed stock control forms for you to fill in; otherwise you can draw one up yourself. Set minimum and maximum stock levels for each product depending on its popularity. Each week or month, count how many you have of each product and how many you think you will need to order. Make a note of the day that this was carried out on the stock control sheet.

 You can double-check if the items were sold by comparing your missing stock to your daily takings book which records all the items sold. If items were not sold then you may have to consider if they were stolen, and tighten up your security methods.

Computerised stock control uses software packages which are available either as stand-alone items or as part of a computerised salon management system. These software systems are multifunction and can be used for a wide range of your salon's management tasks, such as booking appointments. They also help minimise possible thefts of money and stock, and the hiding of appointments.

You can also set up and print simple stock control sheets on any computer by using Excel spreadsheets or a simple Word document. The best method is the one that works for you and your salon.

STOCK ROTATION

Retail products should be checked for their expiry date and damage every time you do a stock take. Some suppliers will accept out-of-date products and in return provide you with new ones, but most make you absorb the loss yourself. To prevent this happening it is good practice to implement stock rotation. This means that new products are placed at the back of the shelf, allowing the older products to be sold or used first.

Products approaching their sell-by date should be reduced in price or put on offer before they become out of date. If you find that there are slower-moving products, then stock levels of these should be reduced to minimum levels or made available for special order only.

If there is no minimum order level and no expensive delivery charge, then ordering products should be done on a regular basis to maintain continuity. Always bear in mind that some companies may take time to deliver, sometimes three to seven working days. We will discuss this further in Chapter 7.

STOCK ARRIVAL

When an order is being delivered, make sure the packaging has not been opened and is not damaged in such a way that the products might have been damaged or taken out. If you have to sign for the delivery, make a note near your signature of any damage or the fact that the contents have not been checked.

Once you have opened the boxes, check the contents against the delivery note, the invoice and what you have ordered to ensure that all items ordered and paid for have actually been sent. If there are any damaged goods or a shortfall, contact the supplier immediately.

New arrivals should be added to your stock control sheet with a note of the date they were delivered. Sometimes shortfalls in your delivery are due to the company being out of stock, which they will generally send you later on. Keep a note of all such shortfalls.

PAYMENT

An invoice is sometimes sent with the delivery or posted at a later date. This form sets out the supplier's name and contact details, your account number and details, the order number which should match the delivery note, details of the order, terms of payment including any discount or terms of credit, carriage charged, VAT and invoice total. The invoice usually needs to be paid within 30 days, although if your business has no previous trading history you may find that suppliers require immediate payment with a credit card before the order is dispatched. A pro-forma invoice is also used for this purpose as it requires the customer to pay for goods before they are dispatched. Once the credit-worthiness of your business has been established, it should be possible to set up an account with your regular suppliers allowing you credit for 30 days or so, which will help with your cash flow.

Making the most of your windows

Hopefully you have been lucky enough to have a window in which to promote your business. Your window display is the 'face' of your salon and will have a great deal of impact on the passing public. Your salon's image, your products and your treatments can all be presented and advertised to thousands of people without one word. Here are some important pointers for window display:

☐ Keep it simple. Uncluttered and uncomplicated displays are the most effective.

☐ Make your window stand out from the rest with a bold colour or design.

☐ Check that you have the balance right by stepping back and looking at your window from outside your salon.

☐ Regularly change the displays to keep interest.

☐ Do seasonal treatment and product promotions.

☐ Be professional in your presentation by avoiding handwritten signs or blutac. It is not expensive to have signs printed and you can store them in an art folder to be used again and again.

☐ Use your product supplier's posters and marketing materials whenever possible.

☐ Pick up ideas from trade fairs and big department stores.

Cancellations and no-shows

Cancelling of appointments by either the therapist or the client is sometimes inevitable due to last-minute dramas and events such as illness, power cuts or family crises. The key is to manage these without causing inconvenience or disappointment to the client, and to minimise the effect on your business.

SALON CANCELLATIONS

If you have to cancel an appointment, be as professional as possible.

☐ Contact the client as soon as possible.

☐ Make sure that you call and talk to the client. If you can't, leave a clear message and call again. Try alternative methods such as texting or sending an e-mail.

☐ Apologise and explain the true reason.

☐ Always offer several alternative appointments, as soon as possible.

CLIENT CANCELLATIONS

Make sure that all clients know the cancellation policy of your salon by informing them at the time of booking as well as on your treatment menu and website. Most salons charge 50% of the treatment price if a client fails to arrive or fails to give 24 hours' notice of cancellation.

Of course, you may need to be flexible in enforcing your policy in cases of genuine emergencies. One drawback to enforcing your cancellation charge rigidly is that the client may be deterred from returning to your salon. One solution to this problem would be to implement any penalties only in cases of persistent offenders, explaining the effect their no-shows have on your business.

Missed appointments or no-shows are a daily annoyance for most service industries such as hairdressers and beauty salons. When an appointment is made, the salon allocates a therapist and sets aside a certain amount of time for that client. Failure to turn up without giving enough notice causes disappointment to other potential customers, loss of other appointments and loss of income to the business. If no-shows are allowed to continue and get out of hand, the financial effect on a small business can be considerable.

To minimise the problem of no-shows:

☐ Ensure all clients know your missed appointment and cancellation policy.

☐ Call clients if they are more than five minutes late, to see if they are still coming.

☐ Keep a cancellation list for other clients requesting an appointment; if a last-minute cancellation arises, call them.

☐ Keep a record of all persistent offenders on clients' record cards.

☐ Remind persistent offenders of their next appointment by phoning them the day before.

☐ Take credit card details at the time of booking and enforce the penalty if appropriate in cases of no-shows.

☐ Explain to the offenders the impact on your business of missing an appointment. Most people understand and will not repeat.

Preventing accidents

Every place of work, including your salon, must have policies and procedures for keeping the place as safe as possible, preventing accidents and knowing what to do when accidents happens. If such policies and procedures are always followed, then accidents involving clients and staff will be eliminated or greatly reduced. Salon safety was mentioned in Chapter 2. However, as part of the salon's management, it is important to go over some essential basic procedures which involve the salon owner, the salon's manager and all the staff.

Some basic procedure for risk assessment would be:

☐ Prepare a list of all treatments, jobs and tasks which will be done in the salon, as well as all the equipment, machinery and products which will be used.

☐ Identify where and how each job is done.

☐ Assess the risk and danger involved with each and every task, job, treatment, pieces of equipment and product used in the salon. The assessment must include danger or risk to the health and safety of clients, staff and yourself, as well as anyone else who might visit your salon.

☐ Prepare a procedure that must be followed which will remove or minimise all hazards and the risk of an accident.

☐ Implement any action to be taken to reduce the risk.

☐ Keep a copy of your risk assessment on file.

☐ Your Health, Safety and Accident Policy and Procedures must be clearly documented and easily accessible and available to all members of the staff.

☐ Ensure that everyone is fully aware of the salon's policies and procedures.

☐ Rigorously implement the procedure which you have put into place.

☐ Revise and review your system regularly or as often as necessary.

☐ Continuously monitor and ensure that your system is being implemented and that everyone uses it. This is often done during staff meetings when the subject is discussed and everyone is reminded of its importance.

☐ Use common sense. If you think something may cause an accident, avoid it.

Never leave loose wires, electric cables or anything that could cause someone to trip over, on the floor. Tape down wires and cables with duct tape as soon as a potential tripping hazard is identified.

Dealing with emergencies

Even when every precaution has been taken to ensure the health and safety of your clients and staff, accidents and illness do happen and it is important to be prepared for any eventuality. Every member of staff should be clear about what to do in case of an accident or emergency or sudden illness.

Ideally, every beauty salon should have a trained first aider on its staff. Many beauty therapy courses include training in first aid as part of gaining the qualification but if this subject has not been covered then first-aid training is available at several colleges and at voluntary health organisations such as the Red Cross and St John Ambulance at a cost of between £100 and £500.

As the owner of a salon, it is worth the investment to go on the training course yourself, or to send another member of staff, as a trained first aider on the pay roll is invaluable for peace of mind in any business dealings with the public. After completion of a short course, a first-aid certificate is awarded with refresher training necessary every three years. For further information, look at www.redcross.org.uk and www.sja.org.uk

Salon policies and procedures must include this very important subject and everyone should read and be aware of its contents. The ideal time to talk about possible incidents and what to do when they occur is during your staff meetings or regular training events, when an hour or so can be allocated to various discussions. It is good practice to write down a basic list of what to do in an emergency, and place it somewhere visible such as in the reception or in the staff room. Do not assume even the most basic of knowledge – some people do not know what to dial to call the emergency services (999).

A first-aid manual is a very useful item to have in the beauty salon for easy reference. There are several excellent ones available with clear diagrams, such as the authorised manual of the St John Ambulance, St Andrew's Ambulance Association and the British Red Cross published by Dorling Kindersley.

A fully-stocked first-aid kit (you can buy a ready-made one at any chemist) should be kept in a convenient and accessible place such as the reception or the staff room. The box should be clearly identifiable (in green with a white cross) and kept clean. It is a good idea to have a sticker placed inside with the phone numbers and addresses of your local accident and emergency department, specialist eye injury department (if you have one nearby), nearest GP surgery and the emergency services number.

The first-aid box should contain the following items, but add to it if required.

☐ Plasters in various sizes.

☐ Individually-wrapped sterile wound dressings (six medium and two large).

☐ Two sterile eye dressings.

☐ Sterile water.

☐ Four individually-wrapped triangular bandages.

☐ Six safety pins.

☐ Instant ice packs.

☐ Two pairs of disposable gloves.

☐ Scissors.

☐ First-aid leaflet.

Note that tablets or medications have not been included in the list as first aiders are not allowed to administer un-prescribed medicines. Even if you know that taking an aspirin or anti-histamine would help the client, you would be very unwise to offer them as you could be opening yourself up to the risk of litigation. Always exercise caution in carrying out first aid as not all patients are grateful for the care that you are giving them.

The following is a list of suggestions that should be followed in case of an accident or sudden illness:

☐ Keep calm and do not panic.

☐ Do not give medication, even basic painkillers.

☐ Don't leave the injured person alone; send someone to phone for help and confirm with them on their return that help is on its way.

☐ Call for trained or professional help immediately.

☐ Dial 999 for the emergency services, giving them the location, phone number and details of the accident and patient.

☐ Keep the patient warm while waiting for help.

☐ If necessary put the patient in the recovery position (**abc**):

   – Clear **a**irways

   – Check **b**reathing

   – Check pulse (**c**irculation)

☐ If the patient has possible neck or back injuries from a fall, do not move them as this could cause further injury.

☐ Do not attempt to do anything beyond your knowledge and training.

Dealing with injuries

Most injuries that are encountered in a beauty salon are usually minor, and mainly one of the following.

Burns are caused by being in contact with a dry heat source, such as a laser or hot wax, or by touching a hot object such as a heater or fire.

Scalds are caused by wet heat such as very hot liquids or steam.

Both burns and scalds cause a reddening of the skin, with possible blisters and weeping. Treatment for both is to cool the area as quickly as possible with cold running water. Blisters should not be burst. Severe burns should be covered lightly with a sterile dressing and the patient taken to hospital.

Cuts, provided they are minor, can be treated with a sterile plaster. More serious cuts should have pressure applied to stop the flow of blood and then a sterile dressing applied. If the cut is deep or the bleeding cannot be stopped, the patient should be taken to hospital.

Bruises, fractures and sprains can all result from a fall in your premises. It is recommended to follow the **RICE** procedure to help reduce the swelling and if necessary seek further help by calling 999.

- **Rest**

- **Ice**

- **Compress**

- **Elevate.**

If the person has hit their head in a fall, they may feel dazed, sick or cold. They may have concussion. Keep the patient warm and seek help. Always be aware of possible head, neck or back injuries if the fall was severe and be cautious about moving the injured person.

Eye injuries can result when a foreign body such as grit or tint enters the eye. To remove the object or tint, either clean the eye with a clean tissue or wash the eye with sterile water and an eye bath. If this fails to work, for all eye injuries cover the eye with a loose sterile dressing and take the patient to the nearest A&E or eye trauma unit.

Fainting can occur if your client is feeling unwell, is pregnant, on a diet, fasting or has been in a hot, stuffy room. Some people feel faint when getting up after a treatment and they should be encouraged to take their time and get up gradually. To restore circulation to the brain, sit the person with their head between their knees until they feel better.

The therapist should always be aware if a client has any pre-existing conditions such as **diabetes, epilepsy, a pacemaker** or **heart condition** and any **allergies**. Always make a note of any health conditions on the client's record card prior to treatment, highlighting them if necessary with a highlighter pen to make sure that everyone is aware if the treatment, such as electrical therapy, is contra-indicated.

KEEPING AN ACCIDENT BOOK

All accidents at work involving employees, visitors or clients should be recorded in detail as soon as possible after the incident. This could be very important in the case of any claim against you arising from the incident or your care. It is also a legal requirement if you have more than ten employees. However, it is strongly advised that you have an accident book no matter what size your business is. You can order an Accident Record Book online or make your own using a simple notebook, clearly marking it 'Accident Record Book'. It should be kept in an accessible place such as near the first-aid box or at your reception.

A record of the accident must include:

☐ Full name of the person involved.

☐ The date and time of the accident.

☐ A short description of the event, including how and where it happened.

☐ The first-aid action taken and by whom.

☐ The signatures of both the manager and the injured party to confirm that the information is accurate.

REPORTING OF INJURIES, DISEASE AND DANGEROUS OCCURRENCES REGULATIONS 1985

If you are an employer or are self employed, you have a legal duty to report any work-related deaths, major injuries, diseases and near-misses that occur at work or on your premises to employees, clients or visitors under the Reporting of Injuries, Disease and Dangerous Occurrences Regulations 1985 (RIDDOR). The information collected allows the Health and Safety Executive to identify where and how injuries in the workplace arise and to investigate any serious incidents. This is particularly relevant to laser clinics where serious and permanent harm can be caused by misuse or malfunction of the machine. Hopefully the reporting of any incidents will be a very rare event for any business.

The Incident Contact Centre can be contacted on 0845 300 99 23 or online at www.hse.gov.uk/riddor

Ensuring fire safety

It is important to consider fire safety and what to do in case of a fire, as a beauty salon has many hazards including flammable materials and electrical equipment. These are very important issues for the salon owner, who has the responsibility of both the safety of their staff and clients, and of the business premises and its contents.

The Fire Precautions Act 1971 and the Regulatory Reform (Fire Safety) 2005 set legal obligations on the employer and salon owner. Under these requirements you must:

☐ Provide a fire escape route for employees and members of the public.

☐ Designate a responsible person to ensure the safety of all people on the premises or who may be affected by fire at the premises.

☐ Carry out regular fire-risk assessments and act on any findings.

☐ Ensure firefighting equipment is working, regularly checked and serviced.

In addition, a fire certificate is required:

☐ If there are 20 or more people on the premises at any one time.

☐ If there are 10 or more people on the premises anywhere other than the ground floor.

☐ If you share your building with other businesses.

The Electricity at Work Regulations Act 1989 specifies ways in which electricity and electrical equipment should be installed, used and maintained in order to prevent injury and fire. An electrical certificate must be obtained from a qualified electrician following an annual safety check, and staff must be trained in the safe and correct use of all electrical items.

Before opening your beauty salon it is vital to carry out a risk assessment and take specialist advice on fire prevention. The action that you will need to take and the firefighting equipment required will depend on the size of premises (how many treatment rooms), location (top floor, ground or basement) and how many people will be on the premises at any one time. This subject is covered further in Chapter 2.

There are four different types of fire extinguisher available. Check with your fire officer or adviser which is most suitable for you.

☐ Red – uses water for paper, wood and textiles.

☐ Cream – uses foam for flammable liquid, paper, wood and textiles.

☐ Black – uses carbon dioxide for dry electrical fires, removing oxygen from the vicinity of the fire.

☐ Blue – uses dry powder for many purposes, including electrical fires and flammable liquids.

You will be advised where your fire extinguishers should be kept and you should make sure that all staff know where they are and how to use them. A fire safety adviser must check the equipment annually to ensure that it is in full working order. Each month a fire safety drill should be carried out to test your fire alarm, your emergency lighting and to train your staff in the safe evacuation of the building. Record this each month in a fire safety notebook with the date, time, test result and who carried out the test, as well as any maintenance of fire equipment. This notebook should be available for inspection by your fire safety officer, local council or insurance company.

Although smaller fires can be swiftly dealt with, there may be an occasion on which the building has to be evacuated. This procedure should be prepared for in advance so that everyone knows what to do if the worst-case scenario happens. The following is a simple plan to follow:

☐ Prepare an evacuation plan.

☐ Train all your staff in the emergency procedure.

☐ If a fire is spotted, keep calm and raise the alarm.

☐ Do not waste time retrieving personal belongings.

☐ Guide all people in the building to the fire exit.

☐ Close doors and windows behind you.

☐ Turn off electrical appliances and lights if possible.

☐ Never use a lift, and always use a designated fire escape route.

☐ Evacuate the building in an orderly manner.

☐ Assemble at a designated meeting point.

☐ Phone 999 for the fire brigade.

☐ Check that all members of staff are accounted for.

Keeping your salon secure

All business owners and shopkeepers must be aware of security in their premises, and the beauty salon is no different. Assess the problem and take preventative action now before the unthinkable happens. Let us consider some of the common problems arising in the salon.

BURGLARY

This is an increasingly common problem in the beauty industry. Consider the amount of expensive equipment and products and the lack of security that is in place in the average salon, and you can see why beauty salons are often seen as an easy target for thieves. The stolen products and equipment are easily sold, leaving the salon owner unable to operate fully, possibly waiting for months for the insurance company to pay out. If you are underinsured then a burglary could mean financial ruin. The following is a list of recommendations to reduce the risk:

☐ Talk to your local crime prevention officer for information and practical advice.

☐ Install window grills if viable.

☐ Install a burglar alarm.

☐ Make sure all windows have locks and that they are used.

☐ Ensure the front and back doors have security glass and two locks, one of which must be a five-lever mortice lock.

☐ Add security lighting to the front and back of the building.

☐ Remove all cash from the premises every night. Put a note to this effect on the door.

☐ Leave your till open so that anyone looking through the window can clearly see that it is empty.

☐ Security mark all expensive equipment with a UV pen.

☐ Remove leads and attachments to expensive equipment such as laptops, and store it separately or take it home with you every evening.

☐ Make sure you are insured for the full replacement cost of your entire stock, professional and retail, and all your equipment in case the worst happens.

THEFT OF PRODUCTS

This is an inevitable part of having a shop and selling products. It is a sad fact that small items and beauty products are a magnet for shoplifters, and add to this the often low level of awareness in the average small salon compared with a large department store and you can see the opportunities there are for thieves. It is not just in reception where products go missing but also in the treatment room and store room. Take the following precautions:

☐ Add closed circuit cameras (CCTV) to cover reception, the till and products.

☐ Keep close tabs on your stock by operating an efficient stock-control system, thereby identifying stolen products at an early stage. Compare what you have in stock at the beginning and the end of a week with what you have sold in that week – the resulting figures and items should match. If not, items are missing.

☐ Keep all valuables, treatment products, expensive equipment and confidential records in a lockable store room or office.

☐ Keep the stock room locked at all times. Theft of wax and other professional use items is commonplace.

☐ Some businesses ban employees from having large bags with them; they allow only one small personal handbag.

☐ Some companies search the bags of all employees when they leave the premises at the end of the day. Consider if this is something you feel happy to implement or not. If you decide to do so, all employees must be searched and treated equally to prevent discrimination or victimisation.

☐ Be very vigilant when two or more people come in and start looking around the retail products, especially if one keeps you occupied with questions away from the others.

☐ Put empty dummy boxes of expensive products on the shelves and windows.

PAYMENT FRAUD

There are several opportunities for deception and fraud when payment is being made. Cheques are the most susceptible unless a strict procedure is followed (see the explanation given in Chapter 9 and earlier in this chapter). Fake banknotes are also a regular occurrence. But card fraud is the most widespread with total losses amounting to over £600 million in the UK in 2008. Cards can be fraudulently used in several ways:

☐ Internet, phone, mail order (customer not present).

☐ Counterfeit (skimmed/cloned) cards.

☐ Lost or stolen cards.

To safeguard your salon, take the following preventative measures:

☐ Take advice from the suppliers of your merchant services (PDQ or card machine). They are taking card fraud seriously and have lots of advice and guidance on how to safeguard your business when handling transactions.

☐ Make sure all staff, not just the receptionist, know the correct procedures for taking cash, cheques and cards to minimise fraud.

☐ Check all larger banknotes with a special Detector Pen Marker or a UV Light Machine which exposes counterfeit notes. Both can be bought from reputable stationery shops.

☐ Keep the note given by the customer outside the till until the change is given. This prevents any doubt on what note the customer gave in the first place.

☐ Train staff to know how to calculate the correct change.

☐ When a large note is given, check the change you are giving back twice.

☐ Never open the till without a transaction, for any reason.

☐ Refunds on products should be authorised only by the manager/owner, and then a procedure must be followed (see earlier in this chapter).

☐ Make one person responsible for the till. Check the balance in the till throughout the day and make sure the till readings and card banking are reconciled at the end of the day.

ROBBERY

Thankfully this is a rare occurrence but it must still be considered and the risk assessed, as a beauty salon is just as at risk as other shops in the High Street. Take the following measures:

☐ Ask advice from your local crime prevention officer.

☐ Install a device that rings or buzzes when the front door is opened, or someone walks in.

☐ Train staff in what to do in an emergency.

☐ Have a panic button installed by your burglar alarm company near the till.

☐ Report any burglary to the police immediately.

THEFT OF CONFIDENTIAL RECORDS

Under the Data Protection Act the employer has an obligation to keep all records and data, whether handwritten or on a computer, safe and confidential. This is especially important if customer card details are taken to secure an appointment or for mail order or internet sales.

It is also possible that employees may take clients' contact details for their own gain or to pass on to other salons if they leave. This can have a devastating effect on a salon if a popular therapist leaves to go to a rival salon, taking a large number of your clients with them.

To safeguard yourself and your business, make sure of the following:

☐ All client record cards, consultation cards and employee files must be kept in a lockable cabinet, preferably in a store room or office which can be locked. The key should be kept by the manager or salon owner.

☐ Do not store card details in a form that can be used.

☐ Buy a shredder and destroy all unwanted confidential documents and information.

☐ Consider putting a clause in your employment contracts preventing employees from working for a rival business within, say, one mile for a period of one year.

☐ Make it clear to employees that obtaining the contact details of clients for their own gain and use, or passing them to others, is a disciplinary offence.

Although all the problems described above sound frightening and overwhelming, do not dwell on them too much. However, you do need to be aware of the issues and how best to deal with them should they arise.

SAFETY OF CLIENTS AND STAFF

The beauty salon owner will be responsible for and need to take steps to safeguard the safety of all employees and customers at all times. Take time to consider vulnerable times and situations – when staff are alone or locking up, clients' belongings when having treatments – and think of ways of making your working environment safer.

☐ Consider providing lockers for staff's belongings.

☐ Don't allow one member of staff to open or close the salon alone; if possible, ensure that there are two members of staff.

☐ Cash up discreetly at the end of the day with the salon doors and windows closed and locked.

☐ Vary the times that goods are delivered.

☐ Vary the times of going to the bank. Avoid taking large amounts of cash and if possible take someone with you.

☐ Never leave one person working alone late at night.

☐ Most thefts are minor in the salon, including cash, mobile phones or jewellery. Discuss these matters with all employees at your staff meeting and ask for suggestions to combat this problem.

☐ Ask clients to put their expensive jewellery in the safe at reception during treatments. Diamond rings going missing is a very common occurrence during manicures.

☐ Put up a sign disclaiming responsibility for any loss or theft on the premises.

Salon management is like juggling – managers need to be able to keep all the balls in the air while remaining calm and smiling! You have to be good at communicating with your clients and with your team, leading by example and managing effectively to push the business forward. Prepare yourself for any eventuality by having procedures in place; your salon will then operate smoothly and successfully.

4

QUALIFICATIONS, TRAINING AND SKILLS

To build a successful beauty salon business you and your staff should know and love the industry that you have chosen to be in. You should take pride in your work and the high professional standards that are expected by clients, and create a beauty business that can be trusted and respected. Obtaining a recognised qualification and having a thorough grounding in both theoretical and practical skills are the first steps towards a long-term professional life that you can be proud of. You will need to continue your knowledge and experience development by continually updating your training and keeping up to date with what is going on in the industry. It is important to network with others in the industry by joining trade associations and attending seminars and exhibitions.

The professional beautician

The profession of beauty therapy has never been so popular and can lead to a variety of career paths, including:

☐ Joining a cruise ship.

☐ Working in a health spa.

☐ Working in a beauty salon or hairdresser's.

☐ Being a mobile beauty therapist.

☐ Teaching.

But perhaps the biggest proportion of qualified beauty therapists aim for, and eventually succeed in, working for themselves. There are more self-employed women in the beauty industry than in any other profession except hairdressing. Part-time or full-time, freelance or employed, nail specialist or all-rounder, there are many opportunities for the qualified therapist.

This is a business that demands that you are caring and professional. So, right from the start make sure of the following vitally important criteria:

☐ Gain recognised qualifications.

☐ Look after your appearance.

☐ Behave professionally with clients and colleagues.

☐ Take care and pride in your work.

☐ Maintain high standards of hygiene and safety at all times.

☐ Continually increase your knowledge by education and training.

What can I study?

There are many courses for all aspects of beauty therapy so the choice is down to your individual needs and interests. There are short courses of one or two days, and part-time evening courses, both of which often cover only one part of beauty such as nails or massage. But before you start any of these short courses, think why you have chosen it. Do you need the qualification to find work? If that is the case, it would be better to undertake a recognised qualification such as NVQ, CIBTAC or ITEC first, as these will be required by any future employer. However, if you are doing it only for your own enjoyment or as an additional skill to your existing qualifications, then these short courses are fine.

Adding skills and techniques to your portfolio will really increase the prospects of success in your career. They will not only enhance your knowledge but will also make you more attractive to an employer in an increasingly competitive job market. And of course if one day you decide to start your own salon, then you are in a much stronger position. There are many areas of specialisation. The following are some of them:

- ☐ Hopi ear candles.

- ☐ Indian head massage.

- ☐ Aromatherapy.

- ☐ Reiki.

- ☐ Micro-dermabrasion.

- ☐ Skin peels.

- ☐ Brazilian waxing using hot wax.

- ☐ Ionithermie.

- ☐ IPL/Laser.

- ☐ Acrylic or gel nails.

- ☐ Tips or nail extensions.

- ☐ Eyelash extensions.

- ☐ Make-up.

To gain a qualification and to start your career in beauty there are several courses and examining boards to choose from, at a variety of schools and colleges, private and state-subsidised. We will examine how to choose a good school later in this chapter, but first let's consider which qualification to choose.

Choosing a qualification

In the UK there are currently several beauty therapy courses that provide recognised training, leading to approved qualifications.

NVQ

National Vocational Training Qualification is the most popular qualification for entering the beauty therapy industry and is the modern equivalent of an apprenticeship. There are numerous colleges around the country offering NVQ training alongside practical experience in a salon with regularly assessed work modules. Some are full-time, while others are part-time or evening. Most of these courses are free or at a modest cost.

NVQ1 and NVQ2 are the two basic entry levels covering manicure, pedicure, waxing, facial massage, make-up, customer care, health and safety and reception duties.

NVQ3 is more advanced and will enable students to gain better employment prospects. This level covers electrolysis, electrical face and body treatments, body massage and artificial nails.

CITY AND GUILDS

City and Guilds is the leading vocational awarding body in the UK, awarding NVQs as well as their own diplomas in beauty. They range from entry levels 1 and 2, to advanced levels 3 and 4 and right up to degree level.

For more information on courses, have a look at the City and Guilds website www.cityandguilds.com

ITEC

ITEC (International Therapy Examination Council) qualifications are recognised internationally and give an excellent practical-based qualification. Courses can be taken full-time, part-time or in the evening. There are currently 12 different diplomas and certificates for beauty, 11 for complementary therapies and more than six for sport and business studies. Diplomas cover subjects such as ear piercing, electrical facial treatments, red vein treatments and IPL.

The courses are available at accredited colleges and schools throughout the UK. Most colleges will charge fees, while others offer nominal or subsidised fees for under 19-year-olds.

For further information, visit www.itecworld.co.uk

VTCT

VTCT (Vocational Training Charitable Trust) is a large specialist government-approved awarding body which offers a wide range of national vocational training and qualifications in the beauty industry. The certificates and diplomas are offered in over 500 further education schools and colleges in the UK and cover all aspects of beauty therapy, nail services, hairdressing, holistic and sports therapies.

The VTCT diplomas and certificates are well regarded and provide first-class vocational training equivalent to NVQ levels 1, 2 and 3, and are recognised by the Qualification and Curriculum Authority.

For further information, visit www.vtct.org.uk

BTEC

BTEC (Business and Technology Education Council) national diploma and certificate in beauty therapy sciences offers a wider study into the more scientific aspects of beauty therapy. For the more academically able, this two-year diploma offers an excellent grounding in both the theoretical and practical sides of beauty therapy and is ideal for those wishing to progress to a degree and improve their career prospects. BTEC National Diploma consists of 720 hours of theory and practical work, while the BTEC Higher National Diploma consists of 1080 hours, and written and practical exams are undertaken at the completion of each module.

This diploma is taught at colleges of further education throughout the UK and if you are over 19 there will be a course fee. However, you may be eligible for student finance and further details of the costs can be obtained from your local colleges or at www.studentfinance.co.uk

FOUNDATION DEGREE AND HIGHER NATIONAL DIPLOMA (HND)

There are several foundation degree courses in beauty therapy which cover the theoretical and practical aspects of a wide range of therapy techniques as well as giving a thorough grounding in the science and in business and financial management. These courses are suitable for therapists wishing to progress to degree level who have already obtained NVQ3, BTEC or equivalent. Although there are no exact 'A' level requirements, selection for places is gained through an interview. Courses available include Salon Management at University College Birmingham, Salon and Spa Management at the University of Plymouth and Foundation degree in Beauty Therapy and Health Studies at the London College of Fashion. There are other courses offered at several colleges and universities throughout the UK. For the most up-to-date information, look at the UCAS website which also handles all application enquiries.

DEGREE

If you would like to continue your education to degree level, there is a limited number of courses available at present. These include BA(Hons) in Spa Management with Hospitality at University College Birmingham and BSc in Cosmetic Sciences at University of the Arts, London.

For further information on all degrees, including foundation, visit www.ucas.com

CIBTAC

CIBTAC (Confederation of International Beauty Therapy and Cosmetology) is the education section of BABTAC (British Association of Beauty Therapy and Cosmetology). It is an international examination with over 150 accredited schools in 18 countries. A CIBTAC Diploma is recognised throughout the world and is renowned for its high level of both practical and theoretical training. In addition, all students must complete a specific number of hours working in a commercial beauty salon environment. The CIBTAC Diploma is a 25-week course followed by theory and practical exams. Many students go on to further study for CIDESCO (see below). The courses are generally run at private colleges and can cost in the region of £7,000 for the full 850-hour diploma or be taken as modules at a cost of approximately £3,000. The main modules are beautician (300 hours), body therapist (300 hours) and electrolysis (200 hours). Other additional modules that are available include reiki, aromatherapy, manual lymphatic drainage, Indian head massage and stress management.

For further information, visit www.cibtac.com

CIDESCO

The CIDESCO (Comité International d'Esthetique et de Cosmetology) Diploma is the most prestigious diploma in the field of beauty therapy. It is held in very high esteem by employers for its highest standards of expertise and professionalism. CIDESCO is a truly international qualification, allowing the therapist to work in over 33 countries around the world. It is a very comprehensive training programme not only in theory and practical experience, but also in developing confidence during training, allowing therapists to gain employment immediately on qualification.

The CIDESCO diploma consists of 1200 hours of study and 600 hours of additional practical work in a commercial salon environment. At the end of this study there are practical and written examinations and a 4000-word thesis. It is also possible to upgrade to a CIDESCO qualification after obtaining another qualification by studying for their Postgraduate Diploma. Other diplomas offered individually include Spa Diploma and the Electrical Epilation Diploma.

Courses are usually offered at private beauty schools and colleges and the full diploma takes between one and two years to complete at a cost in the region of £9,000.

For further information, visit www.cidesco.com

How do I choose where to study?

☐ Decide if you wish to gain a recognised professional qualification or if you just want to do it for enjoyment and skill enhancement.

☐ Choose which qualification suits you best. Are you academic and love studying theory, or are you more suited to practical-based treatments?

☐ Do your research on which schools and colleges are offering which courses. A good source of information is www.habia.org.uk (Hairdressing and Beauty Industry Authority).

☐ Consider what the cost implications are if you want to attend a private college. If you want to study at a state-funded college where the fees will be less, you may be able to secure student finance or a grant.

☐ Compare schools.

– How many students are enrolled on each course and how many staff per student?

– How many students were on last year's course and how many passed?

– Does the course lead to an approved and recognised award?

– Does the centre have a quality rating from an external organisation?

– What are the entrance criteria?

– What is included in the cost of the course (text books, uniform, etc.)?

– Do you need to purchase and use your own equipment during practical sessions? If so, do you have to purchase it through the school and at what cost?

– What products do they use? Dermalogica training while at college will really enhance your employment prospects on graduation.

– How many hours of tuition are received and are home study or case studies required in addition?

– Can you look round the school and meet current students and teachers? Does the school, especially the practical areas, look clean and well maintained?

– Does the school help with careers advice or employment post-graduation?

– Can you enrol at any time or are there set term dates?

– How much are the fees and can you pay in instalments? Is there any funding available?

 One way to find out about beauty schools and courses is to post questions on industry forums such as www.beautyguild.com, www.babtac.com or www.salongeek.com

Further education

Once you have gained your qualification your education must not end there – continue the process of lifelong education. Beauty and holistic therapies are constantly evolving, with new treatments or protocols being added or changing. As professional therapists, we need to adapt our skills and training as products and treatments in our industry advance. We need to take charge of our Continual Professional Development (CPD) to improve our knowledge, skills and competence throughout our working lives. Although CPD is not yet compulsory for therapists, except those working in education, it is considered good practice and will not only enhance the enjoyment of your work but also improve your career prospects.

IMPROVING SKILLS AND KNOWLEDGE

The following is a list of suggestions for improving and broadening your skills and knowledge in the field of beauty therapy.

☐ Take short courses in topics that interest you. Courses of one or two days are a great introduction to new skills and techniques.

☐ Take every possible moment to practise your skills and develop your knowledge. Don't relax just because you have gained your basic qualification.

☐ Read magazines, beauty books and trade journals to find out what is hot in our industry.

☐ Trade journals are essential reading for everyone involved in the health and beauty industry. They are written for therapists by therapists and keep us up to date on new techniques, treatments and important issues. Among the best are *Professional Beauty and Nails, Health and Beauty Salon, Vitality, Scratch, Salon Today, Guild News* and *Today's Therapist.*

☐ Attend trade exhibitions which often hold seminars, lectures and workshops at the same time. These trade shows allow suppliers to showcase new treatments, equipment and products, often at discounted prices. It's a great place for students to buy their first equipment at the best price and for experienced therapists to connect with other therapists and keep abreast of new developments.

☐ Join trade associations. These associations are for people involved in the beauty industry and they regularly run workshops and seminars as well as publishing their own magazines. Look at their websites, which are full of interesting articles and are ideal for keeping up to date on relevant issues and sourcing training courses. At the end of this chapter we have listed the main trade associations and how to contact them.

☐ Use online resources such as web-based forums for the beauty professional. They are a wonderful way of keeping in touch with others and finding out about others' opinions on relevant issues, training courses, products or best practice.

One of the best-known and respected post-graduate training schools in the world is the International Dermal Institute which has 38 schools worldwide. It was founded in 1983 by beauty therapist Jane Wurwand who wanted to improve the quality of training in the beauty industry. At that time there was little to offer the qualified therapist who wanted to gain new skills and further their knowledge of the profession. Jane created a training institute to raise standards and restore pride in the profession by providing first-class learning opportunities for beauty professionals on a wide variety of topics. For further information, visit www.dermalinstitute.com

Training

One of the secrets of running a successful business is having well-trained and knowledgable staff. Your staff are effectively the pillars of your business. Without their strength, knowledge and skills, your business will crumble.

Think about some of the most successful businesses on our High Streets in the UK – McDonald's, John Lewis and Marks & Spencer are a few examples. They are all companies that invest heavily in training their staff. The key advantages to good staff training are:

☐ The staff become more confident in carrying out their work and in offering proper advice to customers. This will result in more sales of the right products or treatments to satisfied customers.

☐ The staff feel valued as professionals within your salon and feel more connected to your business. This will result in job satisfaction, and staff retention creates more loyalty from satisfied customers.

☐ Good training standardises the quality and procedures of each treatment in the salon so that each therapist carries out the treatment in exactly the same way as their colleagues. Customers want standardised treatments so that they can be certain of the same high-quality treatment no matter which therapist in the salon carries it out. This is very important in keeping your customers loyal. Using McDonald's as an example of a very successful business, no matter where you are in the world you know what your Big Mac will look and taste like. You know that you will be served quickly and efficiently and the quality, taste and overall experience will be consistent. That's why we go back, because there will be no unpleasant surprises. The secret of their consistency is the continual training of all their staff, using the company's policies and procedures.

IN-SALON TRAINING

In addition to sending your staff members on training courses to learn new skills, products or techniques, it is beneficial to have regular in-salon training sessions. In-salon training will have the following benefits:

☐ It will create a better bond among your staff.

☐ It will improve staff competence.

☐ You will be able to address issues and weak areas such as sales, booking appointments, customer service, etc.

☐ You can introduce new therapies and products.

☐ It reminds and reinforces salon procedures and standards among the staff.

☐ It will motivate your staff.

Organise in-house training at regular times throughout the year. Prepare for the training session well in advance by considering what you want to achieve. Keep a note of everything you notice that may need some training. Also, make sure during your meetings that your staff discuss what they feel they need training in. Use the feedback you get from your customers regarding the therapist's treatments; this will give you a very good indication of how everyone is operating.

Training is not always about new products or therapies. It is often about refreshing memories on the many things that are taken for granted.

 Before the training session, make sure you have all the necessary tools such as paper, pens, visual aids, DVD or writing board prepared and ready.

The following are some suggestions for your training session:

□ Role play how to overcome a customer's objection to a purchase; practise a few scenarios.

□ Practise answering the phone or welcoming a client into the salon. Make sure everyone does the same.

□ Practise the procedure for dealing with a suspected shoplifter.

□ Role play an accident and make sure everyone knows the procedure that must be followed.

□ Do a fire drill and make sure everyone knows what to do.

□ Carry out a treatment yourself while everyone watches.

□ Get the therapists to work on each other in pairs to learn a new technique.

□ Role play a situation where a customer is not happy and has a complaint. Make sure that everyone knows what to do in such a situation.

□ Repeat the above with a complaint over the phone.

Of course, there are many other things that your staff may need training in. Whatever the training need is, make sure the procedure is consistent for everyone.

Try to make the whole training session fun, relaxed and positive. Be enthusiastic about what you are trying to achieve.

By taking notes throughout the session and getting everyone to participate, evaluate what your staff have learned and achieved from the training session.

OUTSIDE TRAINING

Many beauty product suppliers will do training for you in your salon. Ask your business development adviser what training the company could offer – most do sales training or treatment and product demonstrations. Some companies offer full training in your salon for a minimum number of therapists. This makes life a lot easier than getting several therapists to a venue 100 miles away for a 9a.m. start. Even if there is a charge for this service it may still work out cheaper when you calculate the cost of travel and possibly an overnight stay in a hotel.

Running staff meetings

Regular staff meetings are not only necessary for the smooth running of the salon, but are also very helpful for your staff and your own management.

During staff meetings everyone should be encouraged to talk and contribute to the discussions. You will get the opportunity to hear your staff's concerns and to offer them solutions, while you can point out your concerns and delights with everyone collectively.

 Prepare the topics of discussion *before* going to the meeting, and make sure you take notes of what is said and decided. If there is anything that you cannot answer immediately, reassure staff members that you will look into it and will have a response as soon as possible.

In staff meetings you should:

☐ Emphasise the importance of teamwork.

☐ Keep staff informed as to what's happening in the business and in the industry.

☐ Encourage openness and communication among your staff and the management.

☐ Discuss any concerns, issues or problems which may exist and try to resolve them before they escalate.

☐ Make staff members feel valued and supported.

☐ Discuss incentives and set targets.

☐ Announce the results of previous targets and incentives and give praise where it is due.

☐ Keep complaints against any individual to a general nature (without mentioning any names) and discuss them so that the whole team can learn from any negative customer feedback.

☐ Make sure the staff meeting is the staff's meeting, and that they fully participate.

☐ Listen carefully to what your staff say and make sure they feel you are interested in their views.

Never criticise and never discuss personal issues or an individual's poor performance with any of your staff in public or in front of others at the meeting. It is much more appropriate to handle any problems on a one-to-one basis in private.

Meetings should be held as regularly as possible. Most salons have either a weekly or monthly staff meeting. A very brief daily meeting with everyone first thing in the morning really gets the day off to a good start. If this is not possible, then every effort should be made to at least speak with each member of the team on a daily basis, to go over any queries and to motivate them for the day ahead.

One of the main purposes of holding staff meetings is to make sure that your staff feel valued and listened to. This will result in them feeling much more part of your business and will subsequently help them in wanting to maintain:

☐ Better customer care.

☐ A high standard of personal work.

☐ Improved cleanliness of the salon.

☐ More pride in your salon's image and brand.

 **Remember to keep the tone of the meeting relaxed, positive and fun. Have some sandwiches or pizzas, a drink or a glass of wine; it makes the meeting more relaxed and enjoyable and helps bond the team.**

Offering incentives

Many salons reward staff with weekly or monthly incentives and pay commission on sales and/or services. Staff are generally paid a higher commission on sales (10%) and a lower one on services (5%), and this can really work as a good incentive to achieve sales targets. Other salons offer different incentive schemes such as monthly competitions for the best individual employee's sales, rewarded with a prize or bonus at the staff meeting. Whichever way you reward and incentivise your team make sure that:

☐ The scheme is working.

☐ Clear goals are set within a timeframe.

☐ If you have a target, it is realistic.

☐ The winner or winners are praised for their achievement.

☐ The rewards or prizes are given promptly.

Developing key skills

Some of the key skills that are required for working successfully in the beauty profession, and ultimately running your own beauty business, must have been within you when you first made that decision to choose beauty as your career. Other skills develop during your training, and afterwards when you start your employment or decide to open your own salon.

The following is a list of important skills needed in the beauty therapy industry. If there are any areas where you feel there is a gap in your skills, work on it and ensure you improve.

KEY SKILLS FOR BEAUTY THERAPY

- ☐ Caring in the interest of others in beauty.

- ☐ Friendly and outgoing personality.

- ☐ Enjoy working with people.

- ☐ Hard-working.

- ☐ Good time-management skills.

- ☐ Flexible and adaptable.

- ☐ Able to work as part of a team.

KEY SKILLS FOR BEAUTY SALON MANAGERS

- ☐ Enjoy maintaining high standards in your own work as well as others'.

- ☐ Have effective time-management skills.

- ☐ Have good organisational skills.

- ☐ Be able to delegate and negotiate.

- ☐ Have good leadership skills.

- ☐ Be able to listen and communicate well.

- ☐ Be assertive.

- ☐ Be self-motivated.

- ☐ Have lots of patience!

If you decide to work for yourself and open your own beauty salon, in addition to the above, you will need to:

- ☐ Be an optimist.

- ☐ Have the ability to handle setbacks.

- □ Have high self-esteem.

- □ Be a risk taker.

- □ Remain focused.

- □ Be committed to your aims.

Professional conduct

Professional conduct is taught as part of the basic training to become a beauty therapist. Once you have commenced your training you will be aware of certain standards of behaviour and conduct that you will be expected to conform to. The purpose of this is to maintain hygiene and health and safety of both the therapist and the client, and also to maintain the image of our industry in the eyes of the public as well as your fellow professionals.

The word 'professional' is constantly used in the beauty industry; and here we define and explain what it really means and what it applies to.

APPEARANCE

- □ Clean hair, tied back from the face.

- □ Light, attractive make-up.

- □ No jewellery.

- □ Clean, short and well-manicured nails.

- □ Good personal hygiene.

- □ Clean, ironed and smart uniform.

- □ Always well-groomed.

CUSTOMER CARE

- □ Be respectful of all clients from all walks of life.

- □ Maintain confidentiality at all times.

- □ Treat all clients with understanding and sympathy, be non-judgmental.

- □ Listen to your client's problem rather than talking about your own.

☐ Give every client your undivided attention.

☐ Share your knowledge, and always give honest, unbiased and accurate advice.

☐ Always give the best treatment possible to every client, take pride in your work.

☐ Always be reliable and keep appointments unless due to an emergency.

☐ Don't run late – keep to the appointment time as much as possible.

☐ Maintain proper conduct between client and therapist.

☐ Do not diagnose or treat beyond your professional scope; refer on or up if appropriate.

WITH COLLEAGUES

☐ Never gossip or talk behind people's backs.

☐ Do not negatively criticise other salons, treatments or therapists, remain impartial.

☐ Do not poach clients.

☐ Offer constructive advice rather than negative criticism of colleagues.

☐ Do not undermine a client's faith in another practitioner.

IN BUSINESS

☐ Do not oversell or make false claims regarding results.

☐ Display your treatment prices clearly.

☐ Employ only properly qualified staff and ensure that they are trained.

☐ Do not ask employees to carry out treatments beyond their experience and competence.

☐ Ensure that all staff are fully insured and licensed.

☐ Keep accurate client records and store them in a secure place to maintain confidentiality.

☐ Make sure your premises is a safe working environment.

☐ Make sure all equipment is regularly checked and maintained.

☐ Make sure that you comply with all current legislation, including employment, workplace and health and safety laws.

☐ Always work towards the client's best interests.

PROFESSIONAL ETHICS

All professional associations for the beauty and health industry have their own code of ethics which members must agree to abide by to preserve the high standards associated with the profession. The purpose of this code of ethics is to:

☐ Set out clearly the standards required of the members.

☐ Promote high standards of professional treatments and behaviour within the industry.

☐ Safeguard the public from bad practice.

☐ Enable the public to have confidence in the beauty industry.

☐ Prevent the profession from being brought into disrepute.

Joining professional organisations

Belonging to a professional organisation in beauty therapy is vitally important if you want to build a successful business. These organisations require certain standards of behaviour, knowledge and ethics from their members, thereby maintaining a high professional image that is trusted and respected by both the public and the industry alike. They are non-profit-making and all proceeds are directed to helping promote the beauty profession and giving advice and help to the public.

From a beauty professional's point of view they help us to:

☐ Stay in touch with what's happening in our industry.

☐ Socialise with other members.

☐ Attend exhibitions, workshops and seminars organised by these associations.

☐ Have an ethical and professional code of conduct to abide by.

☐ Give our industry and ourselves a status and a voice.

□ Have discounted services and products such as credit card machines, healthcare or gym memberships.

□ Get access to good-value insurance.

□ Get access to telephone helplines for legal, business or professional advice.

□ Promote beauty therapy to the public.

The following are some of the largest and best-known associations and professional bodies that you should contact and consider joining.

BABTAC (BRITISH ASSOCIATION OF BEAUTY THERAPISTS AND COSMETOLOGISTS)

For over 25 years BABTAC has been the professional face of beauty and holistic therapy in the UK. The association is internationally recognised as one of the longest-running and most influential in the industry. Therapists can apply for membership and their qualifications are assessed to ensure that they meet national and international requirements. BABTAC insists on high standards from its members and is highly vocal in representing the views of its members on relevant topics. It offers members discounts on a variety of products and services, as well as offering insurance policies and legal and business helplines. BABTAC publishes an informative magazine called *Vitality* and has an excellent online forum for members on its website.

Meteor Court
Barnett Way
Barnwood
Gloucester
GL4 3GG

Tel. 0845 065 9000
e-mail. enquiries@babtac.com
www.babtac.com

THE GUILD OF PROFESSIONAL BEAUTY THERAPISTS

The Guild of Professional Beauty Therapists was formed in 1994 and has become one of the biggest associations in the beauty industry, representing over 6000 members. It has a very informative website and bi-monthly magazine to help members keep up to date. The website has an active forum for members to post topics for discussion or to ask advice from other members. Membership benefits include reduced rates for credit card machines and advertising in *Yellow Pages*, and also insurance policies.

Guild House
320 Burton Road
Derby
DE23 6AF

Tel. 0845 21 77 382
e-mail. Louisa@beautyguild.com
www.beautyguild.com

BIAE (BRITISH INSTITUTE AND ASSOCIATION OF ELECTROLYSIS)

The BIAE is a non-profit-making association which was formed in 2004 on the amalgamation of two specialist bodies, The Institute of Electrolysis and the British Association of Electrolysists, which had both been in existence for many years. It has a large membership both in the UK and abroad who are accepted on completion of rigorous theoretical and practical assessments by the BIAE examining board. The BIAE demands a high level of skill and ethical conduct from its members in order to provide a professional and reliable electrolysis service that the public can trust. The association also provides advice and information to the public about electrolysis.

Tel. 08445 441373
e-mail. sec@electrolysis.co.uk
www.electrolysis.co.uk

FEDERATION OF HOLISTIC THERAPISTS

The Federation of Holistic Therapists is the largest multi-disciplinary therapy organisation in the UK and has been representing beauty, holistic and sports therapists for over 45 years. It enforces high professional standards and a code of ethics among its members and encourages Continuing Professional Development by organising seminars and workshops around the country. It offers insurance to its members as well as discounted health plans, leisure schemes, credit card terminals and CRB (Criminal Records Bureau) checks.

18 Shakespeare Business Centre
Hathaway Close
Eastleigh
Hampshire
SO50 4SR

Tel. 0844 875 20 22
e-mail. info@fht.org.uk
www.fht.org.uk

THE COMPLEMENTARY THERAPISTS ASSOCIATION

The Complementary Therapists Association (CTA) is the leading organisation representing over 9000 complementary and alternative medicine therapists in the UK. The association has an excellent website www.embodyforyou.com which runs promotional campaigns with companies such as Müller Lite, *Sainsbury's Magazine* and the *Guardian*, which helped to generate 20,000 potential new business clients for its members.

The CTA also offers reasonably-priced insurance policies for its members as well as a 24-hour legal helpline.

PO Box 6955
Towcester
NN12 6WZ

Tel. 0845 202 2941
e-mail. info@complementary.assoc.org.uk
www.complementary.assoc.org.uk

IPTI (INDEPENDENT PROFESSIONAL THERAPISTS INTERNATIONAL)

IPTI is an independent professional association serving the interests of its members in all forms of therapy, including alternative, complementary, health, fitness and beauty. It provides competitively-priced insurance for its members as well as being a conduit for communication between practitioners.

PO Box 106
Retford
Notts
DN22 1WN

Tel. 01777 700383/703177
e-mail. enquiries@iptiuk.com
www.iptiuk.com

5
STAFF AND EMPLOYMENT

The decision to employ staff should be considered very carefully as it involves increased responsibilities and obligations for you as the salon owner. Finding the right staff to fit into and enhance your team is not easy and takes time but is very important. The staff you will be looking for should be friendly, professional, honest and reliable, and will be a real asset to your growing business. Enlarging your team is essential for your beauty salon to grow, otherwise your business will remain static with you doing everything yourself. All the responsibilities and pressures which that entails will fall on you, so preventing you from managing your business efficiently.

 Don't employ too many people too soon as it can be difficult to terminate someone's employment if business is slow.

Staff can be employed on a part-time, full-time or zero hours contract. They will all need contracts of employment which should be given to them within two months of starting. A sample contract, purely as a guide, is shown in Figure 5.1 (pages 98–101) which should be tailored to meet your own specific requirements.

This document sets out the main particulars of the terms and conditions of employment and also acts as the Principal Statement under the Employment Rights Act 1996.

The parties to the contract:

Beauty Salon Ltd

And

Anne Other

Place of work:

60 High Street, Anywhere AC2 3EF

Date employment commenced: 15 September 20XX

Job title: Beauty Therapist

Job description

> To carry out beauty treatments to a satisfactory standard as required.
> To maintain hygiene, safety and cleanliness in all areas of the salon.
> To promote treatments and sales of products.
> To assist at reception and answer telephone enquiries and appointments.
> To greet clients and maintain high standards of customer service and care.
> To use the till and cash up at the end of day, if and when required.
> To open and close the salon, if and when required.

Normal hours of work

Beauty Salon Ltd hours of trading are 9a.m. to 7p.m. Monday to Saturday.
Total normal hours for each week are 40 hours spread over 5 days. This is based on a rotating schedule with **30 minutes** for lunch each day.
Employees should ensure that they arrive at work 15 minutes **prior** to their start time each morning.

Probationary period

3 months.
Beauty Salon Ltd reserves the right to extend the probationary period, in the hope that a further period will enable you to reach the required standard. A subsequent employment review will be held and a decision made. Your employment will then be either confirmed or terminated with the required notice.

Pay

The rate of pay will be **£XX,XXX** per annum, paid at **£X.XX** per hour.
This is payable **weekly** by **bank transfer** on Saturdays, **one week in arrears.**
Income tax and National Insurance contributions will be deducted from your salary at current UK rates.
After successfully completing the first month, commission (XX%) on product sales will be payable monthly.

Staff treatments

All staff may, at the discretion of the Salon's owner/manager and at a convenient time, have personal beauty treatments at a reduced or zero cost. Prior approval from the owner/manager MUST be obtained; failure to do so may render the employee subject to disciplinary action and payment for the treatment.
Employees may purchase products for personal use at a discounted rate at the discretion of the owner/manager.

Overtime

Employees are required to be flexible and will be required to work a reasonable amount of overtime hours as dictated by customer requirements or as directed by the Company. The rate of pay for overtime is **£XXXX** per hour.

Holiday entitlement

This section sets out your entitlement to holidays, and includes your statutory rights under the Working Time Regulations 1998, which is currently 5.2 weeks per year, *pro rata*.

Your holiday year runs from **15 September 20XX to 14 September 20XX**.
In this period your paid holiday entitlement is **28** days.

The employer reserves the right to make any working day falling between Christmas and New Year, Easter or Public holidays a compulsory holiday, to be taken from your leave entitlement.

No leave, paid or unpaid, can be taken during December.

You must take all your statutory holidays in the holiday year.

Holidays must be agreed in advance with *Beauty Salon Ltd* as early as possible, and *at least twice as much notice as the period of leave to be taken must be given*.
Management will normally try to accommodate individual preferences for holiday dates but the needs of the business may have to take precedence, particularly where inadequate notice is given.

During the probationary period, employees are expected to take leave equivalent only to the amount of leave they have accrued. At the end of your employment you will, at the discretion of the employer, either be paid for accrued leave not taken or be obliged by the employer to take the remaining leave during your notice period. A deduction will be made from your salary for leave taken in excess of your accrued entitlement. If this is insufficient to cover the full amount, the employee will be asked to make other arrangements to pay.

Absence from work

If you are unable to come to work for any reason, you must inform . . . (telephone 0712345678) before 8a.m. on the first day of absence. Failure to do so may render you subject to disciplinary action and may also bar you from any Statutory Sick Pay (SSP).
If the reason for your absence is sickness, you must provide *Beauty Salon Ltd* with a sick note from your GP to retain any eligibility you may have for SSP.
In notifying *Beauty Salon Ltd* you should indicate the reason for your absence and its likely duration.

►

Absence because of sickness

All days of absence because of sickness must be covered by a medical certificate. Because of the rules relating to the payment of SSP (details below) it is important that your certificates indicate actual days of sickness even if they are sometimes days when you would not have worked, e.g. weekends and public holidays.

Most employees will be entitled to SSP in accordance with the rules laid down by law. The main qualifications are that you have done some work under this contract and that you earn the Lower Earnings Level (LEL) in force at the time. You also need to be absent on 'qualifying days', i.e. days on which you would normally be expected to work. The first three qualifying days of absence do not attract SSP.

Pensions

The employer does not provide a pension scheme and there is no contracting out certificate under the Social Security and Pensions Act 1993.

Deductions

The employer may deduct from your salary or other sums due to you, an amount to cover losses sustained in relation to property or money of the employer or of any client, customer, visitor or other employee during the course of your employment caused through your recklessness, carelessness or negligence or through breach of the employer's rules or any dishonesty on your behalf.

The employer may also deduct from your salary or other sums due to you, a day or part day's pay for any unauthorised absence. Unauthorised absence is failing to appear for work at the appropriate time or absence during your normal working hours, unless due to genuine sickness notified to the employer in accordance with the contract, or leave for which prior permission has not been granted.

The employer may also deduct the amount of any accidental overpayment to you, and/or the amount of any loan made to you. The employer will notify you in writing the details of any deduction.

The employer will also deduct the cost of any training courses, and all associated costs, taken by the employee during the course of their employment if the employee leaves, for whatever reason, within one year of the commencement of employment.

Notice

If you wish to terminate your employment with *Beauty Salon Ltd*, you are required to give **one week's** notice in writing to . . .

Should *Beauty Salon Ltd* wish to terminate your employment, for reasons other than gross misconduct, you will be entitled to notice as follows:

Period of service	Notice from the company
During your first month	*none*
After one month's service	*one week*

ConfIct of opportunity, non-solicitation and non-competition

Business opportunities similar to or related to the employer's business that come to the employee's attention while an employee of the Company, will belong to the employer. This clause also prevents an employee competing for trade or business while employed by *Beauty Salon Ltd.*

The employee shall not induce other employees or clients to leave *Beauty Salon Ltd* or interfere with the employer's relationship with other employees or clients in general.
The employee shall not solicit the contact details of clients of *Beauty Salon Ltd* for personal gain. Doing so may result in disciplinary action being taken. The employee is prohibited from being involved with a business in direct competition with *Beauty Salon Ltd* within a 1 mile radius for a period of 1 year.

Confidential information

The employee shall not disclose private or confidential information belonging to the employer, customers, clients or visitors.

Beauty Salon Ltd does not accept responsibility for employees' personal belongings or items while on the premises. All personal items should be kept in the store room which is to be kept locked at all times.

Disciplinary procedures

The disciplinary and grievance procedure in relation to your employment is attached but does not form part of this contract. Employees are required to read the **Salon's Clinic Registry** which contains general rules, guidelines, policies and procedures for employees in all matters relating to their employment.
If you have any matters relating to your employment you should raise them with
_____ (telephone _____).

Personal data

For the purposes of administration, it is necessary for the Company to hold and process personal data on its employees. The data will be held for the duration of your employment or for any longer period to enable the Company to answer any question relating to you as an employee.
Every care is taken to ensure that this personal data is held in confidence and secrecy. You have the right to review and, if necessary, update your personal details on an annual basis. If your personal circumstances change at any time you should inform . . . accordingly. This will ensure that the information remains accurate.

Signed on behalf of *Beauty Salon Ltd* _____
Name and job title:
Date:

I agree to the terms and conditions of this contract, and acknowledge that I have received a copy.

Employee's Name _____ Signature _____ Date _____

Figure 5.1 Sample of a simple contract of employment

Renting a room

One low-cost option that is common practice in the beauty industry is renting a chair or room within your salon to a self-employed therapist or nail technician. While this can provide additional services to your salon without all the usual obligations on an employer, always bear in mind that when this person leaves, many of their clients may go with them. It is very important that this person has registered with the Inland Revenue as self employed and can fulfil the criteria that define this status. And always make sure that you have this confirmed in writing for your records. It is also essential that you have a contract for services provided by the self-employed person. This is different from a contract of employment that you would have with an employee. There are two very good websites which can give you additional information and advice – www.businesslink.gov.uk and www.hmrc.gov.uk

 Make sure that the person renting the room is fully insured for the treatments that they are providing, and is registered with the Inland Revenue as self employed.

Job roles

Every member of your staff should have a clear and defined role. They should know what their job entails and what is expected of them. As the owner of the salon, you are responsible for ensuring that everyone does what they are meant to do and does it properly and professionally.

RECEPTIONIST

The receptionist has probably the most important role in the salon. They are the person who is the 'face' of your business and their skills are vital in the smooth running of your salon. How they answer the phone and welcome clients into your business will create a lasting impression, good or bad. When you advertise for a receptionist you will always get a very high response from job seekers as everyone thinks it's an easy job that anyone can do. It is generally thought that it entails sitting at a desk, painting your nails, reading *Hello!* magazine with the occasional interruption of the phone ringing. Nothing could be further from the truth. What often happens in reality is that a customer is waiting to pay, another customer walks in and wants to buy products, the phone is ringing and the therapists are running late and need assistance.

Your receptionist must be a calm, well-spoken and organised person who can multi-task while keeping a smile on their face.

THERAPIST

A therapist who offers different skills can increase the services you offer. Apart from the usual treatments that most therapists can do, Hopi ear candles, reflexology or gel nails are all popular additional services. Think whether you want to employ a junior therapist whom you can train or someone with experience. Both have their plus and minus points. On the one hand, you will have to invest time, money and energy into training someone at the start of their career who may leave just as you have got them to your standard. On the other hand, a junior therapist may be more open to your way of working and more flexible in their approach. A senior therapist may have years of experience, work much quicker and therefore will be able to do far more clients in a day. However, they may have fixed ideas of how they carry out a treatment, which may not be how you want the treatment to be done. Both drawbacks can be overcome with clear treatment guidelines and an ongoing training programme for all staff.

Finding the right person

Your staff can work full-time, part-time, temporary or freelance. Depending on your requirements, each one of these can be beneficial at certain times and will have its own pros and cons.

THE PROS AND CONS OF FULL-TIME STAFF

Pros

- ☐ Employees work regular hours and days

- ☐ They offer consistency for both customers and other staff in the salon

- ☐ They are generally more dedicated and loyal to the business

Cons

- ☐ Too many staff when the business is quiet such as in the mornings

- ☐ Lack of flexibility to reduce staff during quiet periods

PROS AND CONS OF PART-TIME STAFF

Pros

☐ More flexible, as staff can work when the salon is busy and not when it is quiet

☐ If one member of staff is off due to sickness or holiday, a part-timer may be able to cover by working an extra day or two

Cons

☐ Having more part-timers requires more organisation

☐ It can work out more costly, due to increased insurance costs and additional payroll and National Insurance liabilities

PROS AND CONS OF FREELANCE STAFF

Pros

☐ Can be called in as and when required or are available on specific days and times, giving greater flexibility

☐ Usually specialise in a therapy or skill, often with their own client base

☐ Reduced costs related to their employment as they are self employed and pay their own tax, National Insurance and treatment insurance costs

Cons

☐ Lack loyalty to your business

☐ When they leave, so do their customers

☐ You must adhere to strict guidelines laid down by the Inland Revenue regarding freelancers

PROS AND CONS OF TEMPORARY OR AGENCY STAFF

Pros

☐ Can be called in at very short notice to cover occasional staff sickness and holidays or employed on a short-term contract to cover the busy summer months or Christmas

☐ Limited employment liability and costs depending on whether they are employed by a temp agency or not

☐ Very flexible as the needs of your business contract or grow

Cons

☐ Lack loyalty to your business

☐ Lack of consistent, familiar staff for your customers

☐ Variable standards of work and unfamiliarity with your way of working

As one of the most important parts of your salon operation is to have the right staff, recruitment should be well planned. This is not something that should be done quickly. Writing everything down is a good way of clarifying your thoughts. There are two parts to employing someone. First what the job role is, then what sort of person you need to do the job. It is therefore very useful to have a good written description of the duties the job involves, followed by another list of what qualities, experience and skills are needed for the job.

The following is a set of guidelines which you can follow in your selection process:

1. Establish what you need from the person you want to employ.

2. Write down a list of qualities, training, skills and experience that you expect from your ideal person.

3. Write down the job description (job role) and include all the duties involved.

4. Place your advert, emphasising the most essential skills and qualities and mentioning what would be desirable.

5. Make your first selection from the replies and arrange first interviews.

6. Shortlist the strongest candidates and arrange second interviews.

7. Arrange a trade test.

8. Discuss and select the strongest candidate.

9. If, and only if, you are satisfied, offer the job, emphasising all the major points of the contract.

Examples of job specifications are given in Figures 5.2 and 5.3.

This job involves the following duties:

Answering the phone
Making client bookings
Taking cash and credit card payments
Organising other members of the team throughout the day
Time management of clients and staff
Stock taking
Maintaining a clean and tidy salon and reception
Greeting and welcoming clients and visitors
Changing window displays
Selling and promoting products and sales
General administration

Qualifications/qualities required:

Good spoken and written English (E)
Good interpersonal and communication skills (E)
Able to work under pressure (E)
Good organisational skills (E)
Ability to deal with difficult people and situations. Calm/capable (E)
Happy, outgoing, friendly personality (E)
Clean, groomed and presentable (E)
Retail/hospitality/reception experience (E)
Interest and knowledge of beauty treatments and products (D)
Flexible and adaptable (E)
Able to work evenings, weekends, alternate days (D)

E : Essential
D: Desirable

Figure 5.2   Job specification for a receptionist

 Keep a copy of all job specifications in your salon file and update them as and when required, as well as a record of all your adverts for future reference.

Therapists and staff can be recruited by means other than advertising. One possibility is word of mouth. Putting the word out to all your friends in the industry often turns up a gem and saves you the cost of advertising.

If you are looking for a junior therapist whom you could train, then the beauty schools near your salon are a great source of new talent.

This job involves the following duties:

Carring out beauty treatments to a satisfactory standard
Maintaining hygiene, safety and cleanliness in all areas of the salon
Promoting treatments and sales of products
Answering the phone and assisting on reception when required
Making client bookings
Taking cash and credit card payments when required
Cashing up and reconciliation at the end of the day when required
Opening and closing the salon when required
Maintaining a clean and tidy salon and reception
Greeting and welcoming clients and visitors
Maintaining high standards of customer care and service

Qualifications/qualities required:

CIDESCO, BTEC, ITEC, NVQ3 (E)
Minimum of two years' experience (E)
Confident and skilled in the use of hot wax for Brazilian and Hollywood (E)
Good spoken English (E)
Good interpersonal and communication skills (E)
Ability to work under pressure (E)
Good organisational and time-management skills (E)
Calm, capable, confident (E)
Happy, friendly personality (E)
Clean, groomed and presentable (E)
Knowledge of Dermalogica, Karin Herzog, IPL, Skinceuticals (D)
Flexible and adaptable (D)
Able to work a rota including evenings, weekends, Sundays (E)

E: Essential
D: Desirable

Salary £xxxxx to £xxxxx, depending on experience
xxxx hours per week
Commission on sales and treatments
Personal treatments free/discounted
Discount on products purchase
Uniform supplied
Flexible working hours and pattern
Holiday pay

Figure 5.3 Job specification for a beauty therapist

 Contact your local beauty college head to find out about their top students and snap up the new talent straight from their college.

Sometimes your local beauty supplier or wholesaler will have a notice board to place an advert for staff. Although not very effective, you may just be lucky and find someone this way.

Recruitment agencies will also help find your ideal person from their database and will only forward to you suitable candidates. This saves you valuable time sifting through lots of CVs, most of which could be unsuitable. However, agencies do charge for this service and the fee could be quite high. If they are successful in placing a candidate with you, the commission charged is usually a percentage of the candidate's first-year salary.

The commission charged by recruitment agencies is often negotiable, especially if you use them on a regular basis.

Advertising for staff

If asking around does not turn up anyone suitable and you don't want to pay the big fees to recruitment agencies, then advertising is your only option. There are several trade magazines read by people in the beauty industry including *Guild Gazette*, *Vitality* and *Professional Beauty*. Advertising in these is often expensive, and as they are nationally distributed is not recommended. The most common and probably cost-effective way of recruiting is the online web-based advertising agencies. These often bring a large, rapid and more successful response. Sites to consider include: www.hairandbeautyjobs.com, www.beautyjobsonline.com, www.leisurejobs.com and www.gumtree.com

THINGS TO CONSIDER WHEN WRITING A JOB ADVERTISEMENT

☐ Make it eye-catching.

☐ Use your logo and pictures of the salon. A picture of your happy employees is also effective.

☐ Clearly state the job title, job role and what the job entails.

☐ State which qualifications are required, e.g. NVQ 2 or 3, CIDESCO.

☐ Explain what you are looking for, e.g. experienced, junior, can work independently, and any skills or product knowledge that you require.

☐ State the hours, pay, holiday and conditions.

☐ Include any other condition or benefit you are offering.

There are several pieces of legislation that you will have to be aware of when advertising and recruiting staff. Make sure that you fully comply with them:

☐ The Sex Discrimination Act 1975

☐ The Race Discrimination Act 1976

☐ The Disability Discrimination Act 1995

☐ The Age Discrimination Act 2007

YOUR IDEAL CANDIDATE

In an ideal world, your perfect employee will have all or as many of the following attributes as possible; of course, this will never be the case. But look for these and see what you can get.

☐ Good time-keeping

☐ Reliability

☐ Cleanliness

☐ Loyalty

☐ Commitment

☐ High standards

☐ Well spoken

☐ Pleasant and polite

☐ Team player

☐ Professional

☐ Responsible

☐ Honest

☐ Qualified

□ Well skilled

□ Experienced.

Selecting for interview

When you have received the applications for the job you have advertised, take the time to read the CVs carefully and divide the candidates into three categories.

1. Strong and potentially good applicants.

2. The possibles and maybes.

3. The ones who are totally unsuitable.

Compare the first two groups of applicants with your job description Call the first two groups of candidates and conduct a short telephone conversation. Ask them some simple questions about their experience and skills and what they are looking for, and write down their replies. This gives you an opportunity to hear them speak and will help you to clear up any misunderstandings with their CVs, and eliminate the more unsuitable applicants.

 When inviting candidates for an interview, make sure you ask them to bring their passport, visa (if relevant) and the originals of their qualifications certificates. This is vitally important to verify nationality, right to work in the UK and the authenticity of qualifications.

The interview

Ideally each candidate should be interviewed by at least two people, including the salon owner, business partner or a senior therapist. Using an 'Interview Topics for Discussion' form similar to Figure 5.5 (on page 112), go through each topic and discuss them with the candidate, while recording your views and any comments made on a form similar to that of Figure 5.4 (on page 111). This ensures that you cover all of what you want to talk about and ask the candidate.

An application form should be filled in prior to the interview, and passports and certificates checked.

Job role _____

Candidate's name _____

Retail/hospitality experience _____

Reception experience _____

Beauty experience _____

Hot wax skills _____

Special skills _____

Communication skills, written/oral _____

Ability to manage salon day-to-day _____

Work under pressure, multi-task _____

Time-keeping _____

Numerate/use of till _____

Appearance _____

Motivated/enthusiastic _____

Flexibility to cover _____

Sickness/holidays _____

Holidays booked _____

Travelling distance/method/any special needs _____

References _____

Figure 5.4 Interview notes

Start by putting the candidate at their ease and outline the company history, the types of treatments offered and the ethos. Encourage the candidate to talk about their CV, skills and experience relevant to the job they are applying for. Allow the candidate time to think and speak. The more a candidate talks, the better you get to know them.

You could include the following questions at the interview:

Job role _____

Duties _____

Hours/rota _____

Weekly/monthly pay _____

How and when paid _____

Lunch and tea breaks _____

Holiday pay _____

SSP _____

Appearance/uniform _____

Training, incentives and commission _____

Passport and visa (if applicable) _____

Photos _____

Bank account details _____

Qualifications/certificates _____

Registration with local authority _____

Customer care, loyalty and confidentiality _____

Trade test _____

Other _____

Figure 5.5   Interview topics of discussion

☐ What part of beauty therapy do you enjoy most? Or least?

☐ Why did you leave your previous job?

☐ How would you deal with a customer at the reception area who is making a complaint about her treatment while at the same time another customer is waiting to pay?

☐ Have you ever used a till or handled money?

☐ Do you have any retail experience and do you enjoy selling products?

☐ How long does it take you to do a half leg and bikini wax?

☐ What motivates you?

☐ What is your career aim?

☐ What are your strengths and weaknesses?

☐ Why did you apply for this job?

Using an interview form similar to that of Figure 5.5, take notes of your conversation. This will give you a clear record to refer to later when you have to make your final choice of candidate.

Be aware of any possible discrimination in the questions that you ask which could result in missing the best candidate or leave you open to allegations of unfairness.

Ensure that all aspects of the job role are explained and that the candidate is fully aware of the standards expected. For example, make clear if the job entails working with other members of staff to keep all areas of the salon clean or if the candidate will be expected to take sole responsibility for the salon in your absence or if they would be expected to carry out treatments on men.

Also, give a full explanation of the pay, holiday entitlement and any conditions of employment such as the probationary period and obtaining satisfactory references.

At the end of the interview ask the candidates if they have any questions. Inform them of the possibility of a second interview, trade test and estimated timescales.

It is good practice to keep a written record of all the topics discussed and any comments made on your interview form and attach them to the candidate's CV for ease of retrieval. These should be kept for at least six months in case of subsequent queries.

SHORTLISTING AND SECOND INTERVIEW

After first interviews, a shortlist of two or three of the most suitable candidates should be made and those candidates invited for a second interview. Again, it is useful if the interview is conducted by two people, preferably the original two.

At this interview, your questions should be more work-related and the candidates should be shown around the salon and encouraged to ask as many questions as possible.

One subject that needs to be fully discussed and agreed is the cost of training and product courses. Training for treatments in the use and sale of new products is often needed by new staff. The question is who pays for these and on what conditions. Generally speaking, most salons pay the training course fee and wages for the training days. But in many cases the employee will have to pay back these costs if they leave within the first year.

Once training has been discussed and agreed, make sure that the terms are clearly stated in the contract of employment. This enables the employee to gain the required training without a possibly prohibitive financial outlay and the employer to benefit by gaining a fully-trained member of staff yet limiting the risk of having to pay for training new staff every few months.

Compare your original list of requirements with what the candidates offer.

Arrange a trade test and see how the candidates get on.

TRADE TEST

With all jobs that require an element of skill, a trade test, either after the second interview or on a later day, is common practice. The prospective candidates would be given a work-related task to demonstrate their skill, such as a manicure, pedicure, leg wax, massage or specialist waxing such as a Brazilian with hot wax.

 Remember to take interview nerves into account when assessing work.

Selecting your candidate

At the end of this process, fully discuss all aspects of the final two or three candidates with appropriate colleagues and decide which one fits best with your requirements. References from the successful candidate's last two employers should always be asked for and obtained. All offers of employment must be conditional on satisfactorily completing a probationary period (commonly three or six months) and on obtaining satisfactory references.

The successful candidate should then be contacted and an induction day arranged.

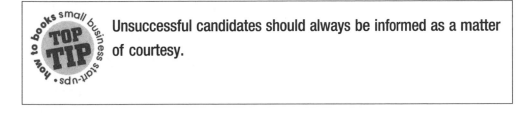 **Unsuccessful candidates should always be informed as a matter of courtesy.**

Induction day

An induction day is important to the smooth introduction of a new member of staff to your salon. Firstly introduce your new member of staff to other members of the team and show them round the salon, where things are and how they work. Explain the ethos of the salon, standards expected in client care and review your treatment list. The therapist should be allowed time to practise these treatments on other members of staff or volunteers prior to treating paying customers.

 It is good practice to standardise your treatments with a set routine which is written down and kept in the salon file.

The standardisation of treatments reinforces your company brand and reassures clients that they will receive the same high-quality treatment on each visit, irrespective of the therapist.

 Use the induction day to go over the very important issues of customer care procedures, standards of cleanliness and the sterilisation and safety routines in the salon.

Unless you employ a full-time receptionist and the post is covered every day of the week, all therapists should be shown how to calculate the client's bill, the operation of the till and how to answer the phone correctly in case they ever need to cover the reception. All members of staff must know what to do in case of fire, accident or other emergencies.

 General staff rules including health and safety guidance should be available in a booklet, easily accessible. Make sure that all members of staff read it and know where it is kept.

The induction day is also the ideal time to deal with all the employment paperwork. Make sure that all the following are dealt with:

☐ The application form is fully filled in.

☐ You have received satisfactory references from the last two employers.

☐ Copies of the new employee's passport, visa (if relevant) and qualifications are provided.

☐ A P45 or P46 has been brought in.

☐ Professional insurance has been arranged for the new therapist.

☐ If required, application for registration for special treatments/massage with the local council has been sent off.

Contract of employment

A contract of employment is a written document stating the main terms and conditions of employment between the employer and employee and should be given within two months of the start of employment. An example of such a document is shown in Figure 5.1.

The contract must include the following:

☐ The legal name of the employer and address of workplace.

☐ The name of the employee.

☐ Full job description.

☐ Date employment commenced, and the period of employment if applicable.

☐ Rate of pay and how it is paid, weekly or monthly.

☐ Normal working hours and overtime requirement.

☐ Holiday entitlement.

☐ Length of notice period for both parties.

The employment contract should be signed and dated by both parties and a copy kept by each for their records.

A contract of employment can be one of the following types:

☐ Open-ended or permanent contract which can be terminated only by giving the notice stated in the contract.

☐ Fixed-term contract which automatically ends after a certain period of time (e.g. one year).

☐ Short-term contract for three months or less.

Both fixed-term and short-term contracts are renewable at the end of the contract. However, if the employee is offered repeated short-term contracts by law this will be regarded as continuous employment.

 To avoid discrimination make sure that you are offering the same terms, conditions and benefits (*pro-rata*) to all staff regardless of whether they are full-time or part-time or on permanent or short-term contracts.

PAYE and National Insurance

As an employer you are responsible for PAYE and National Insurance of all your staff, except those who are self employed. If your wages are looked after by your accountant or book-keeper, then everything will be taken care of. Otherwise, you must:

☐ Inform the tax office when a new employee starts.

☐ Set up a payroll record or P11 Deductions Working Sheet for each employee.

☐ Deduct tax and National Insurance from your employee's wages.

☐ Pay the tax deducted to the Inland Revenue monthly.

☐ Pay the employee's National Insurance contributions together with the employer's contribution to HMRC monthly.

☐ Issue a P45 when an employee leaves and a P60 at the end of the tax year.

☐ Inform the Inland Revenue when an employee leaves.

Sick pay and maternity leave

As an employer, you will also be responsible for paying Statutory Sick Pay (SSP) to employees who are unable to work due to illness and who meet certain qualifying conditions. Firstly you must check if your employee qualifies and, if so, pay the SSP in the same way and at the same time as wages. You will be able to claim back most of the SSP each month from your NI or tax payments.

An employee who is expecting a baby may be entitled to Statutory Maternity Pay (SMP) which replaces her normal earnings around the time of the birth. Whether an employee qualifies for SMP or not depends on the length of service and the wages. However, all female employees are eligible for 26 weeks of ordinary maternity leave, and 26 weeks of additional maternity leave making a total of one year, no matter how recently they have started work for you as long as they have given you the correct notice. Other employer obligations include the payment of Statutory Paternity Pay (SPP) and Statutory Adoption Pay (SAP) if an employee qualifies under certain rules. Once again you should be able to claim back part or all of the SPP, SAP or SMP from the Inland Revenue. For more up-to-date information check the Inland Revenue website at www.hmrc.gov.uk

Many small businesses find these matters complicated and time-consuming, and often the simplest way would be to pay an accountant or payroll service to deal with them for you.

 **Get several quotes from different payroll services and accountants as the charges can differ considerably, and cutting costs for this essential service will help your business's cash flow.**

There are also several software options available for your computer if you want to do the calculations yourself, and a list of approved software can be found on www.hmrc.gov.uk/ebu/acclist.htm HM Revenue and Customs have a specialist helpline for small businesses called HMRC Payroll Support Team on 0845 915 9146.

 Remember that it is a legal requirement to provide your staff with itemised pay slips showing their hours, wages, extra payments and deductions.

Keeping an employee file

Each member of staff should have a separate personal file containing:

- ☐ Letter of application.

- ☐ CV.

- ☐ Interview notes.

- ☐ Copies of passport, visa (if required), qualifications and professional insurance certificate.

- ☐ Records of any complaints by customers.

- ☐ Notes concerning standard of work (good or bad).

- ☐ All disciplinary and grievance procedures fully and accurately recorded.

 You should make sure that all files are securely stored to ensure data protection and confidentiality.

The salon file or staff file

The salon file, also referred to as the clinic file or staff file, is a comprehensive file containing all your salon's rules, regulations, policies and procedures, including those of recruitment, appointment and dismissal, information regarding health and safety, accident, fire alarm and emergency, police and other useful telephone numbers.

This file should be kept in the staff room or another easily accessible place such as near the reception counter where all members of your staff have easy access to it, are aware of it and can read its contents.

 It is good practice to have a signature page that staff can sign and date to say that they have read the file.

Salon rules, policies and procedures

Every business will have its own rules, policies and procedures. These will all depend on the type of business, products and services offered and the people who run it, as well as the various statutory laws and regulations.

SALON RULES

It is recommended that your salon's rules and policies contain the following:

☐ Staff personal treatments: consider whether they are free, at a reduced cost or have an allocation according to work or sales performance, as well as whether staff need to ask permission and/or have the treatments in their own time (i.e. off days, lunch time or after work).

☐ Phone calls: whether personal phone calls are allowed or not.

☐ Presentation: all staff should be well groomed and have high standards of hygiene. Consider whether staff must have clean hair tied back off their face and if they are allowed to have nose studs or wear jewellery while working.

☐ Uniforms: are they to be provided or are the staff required to wear their own uniform?

☐ Starting time: it is good practice to ensure that all staff are on the premises 15 minutes before their start time to avoid unexpected transport delays.

☐ Lunch breaks and rest breaks: clarify how long these are and if the time is flexible. For example, lunch breaks may not necessarily be at 1p.m. every day and may have to be changed according to customer bookings.

☐ Product purchases: do staff get a discount and if so, how much?

☐ Client contact details: rules on obtaining client contact details for the staff's personal use and gain are very important as therapists can build up a client base of your customers by doing mobile work in the client's home while working for you. This must be banned otherwise your business will suffer a loss of customers.

☐ Socialising with clients: this is also an important issue which can often cause problems and possibly loss of clients. Most salons and a lot of businesses ban this and it is well worth you considering it.

☐ Friends and family treatment: treatments for staff's friends and family must be clearly explained and regulated. Decide if you are willing to offer free or discounted treatments and how much and how often. Do they get permission from the owner of the salon or the salon's manager? Allowing this to get out of hand could become a major issue. You could walk into your salon on a normally very busy Saturday and find low takings owing to the staff being busy waxing their friends at no charge.

☐ Beware! Cover all eventualities no matter how minor or unlikely they seem.

 Make clear to everyone the repercussions of breaching salon rules and to what extent disciplinary action against misconduct or gross misconduct could be taken.

POLICIES AND PROCEDURES

If you employ four or more staff, a file containing your policies and procedures is essential. But even if you are starting out on a smaller scale it is a good idea to give these documents some thought and to put something in writing to cover any eventualities. All of these policies must be non-discriminatory and should take into account the relevant legislation. Time spent drawing up this Staff File will pay dividends if you ever receive complaints and are in the unfortunate position of facing the Employment Tribunal. It also helps and supports your staff to know what is expected of them, giving them a framework to operate within and who to talk to to resolve any queries or problems they may have in their employment.

The following list covers the most important topics that should be included in your file of policies and procedures:

☐ Health and safety policy

☐ Risk assessments

☐ Equal opportunity statement of intent

☐ Confidentiality policy (including data protection)

☐ Recruitment policy and procedure

☐ Induction procedure and checklist

☐ Training policy

☐ Staff disciplinary procedure

☐ Staff grievance policy and procedure

☐ Staff dismissal procedure

☐ Staff appraisal procedure together with checklist and forms

☐ Sick leave policy and procedure

☐ Leave policy and procedure, to include holidays, sabbaticals and family emergency leave

☐ Maternity, paternity and adoption policy and procedure

☐ Redundancy policy

☐ Exit interviews

There are specialist human resources companies or employment lawyers who, for an annual fee, can help you with these documents and employment contracts. This can save a great deal of time and worry as employment has become a legal minefield. The issues raised above must be addressed and *not ignored* or you could easily fall into a trap and find yourself facing the legal tangles of the Employment Tribunal. Try your beauty trade associations, such as The Guild or BABTAC, for recommendations.

Staff appraisals

Holding regular appraisals with your staff has many benefits.

☐ They will monitor and assess the individual's performance.

☐ They assess job satisfaction.

☐ Training requirements are identified.

☐ They will give an early indication of any problems or issues.

☐ They improve communication and understanding within the team and with management.

☐ They identify goals and help targets to be achieved.

☐ They will keep staff motivated.

Appraisals should be done in private, in a quiet room and in a friendly and unhurried atmosphere. Both the salon owner/manager and the employee should be relaxed, open and honest. The tone should be positive, with good communication. If any weaknesses, complaints or problems with the standard of work have been identified you should present the facts calmly, ask for reasons and listen to the answers. Try to identify the reasons behind the problem and together look for possible solutions. Try to remain supportive and objective at all times. For example, if a therapist is constantly late for work in the mornings, find out if the journey is subject to frequent delays or maybe the therapist has a very long and difficult journey into work. One solution may be to allow a later starting time in the mornings if this fits into the needs of the business.

As an employer you should be able to:

☐ Discuss the strengths and weaknesses of the employee calmly and objectively.

☐ Identify and discuss training needs to suit both the employee and your business.

☐ Improve communication with your staff and take an interest in them as individuals.

☐ Set targets and goals for the future.

☐ Offer constructive help, advice and praise for your employee.

☐ Agree on an action plan.

An employee should be able to:

☐ Discuss openly and freely any grievances with their employer.

☐ Discuss career aims and future training needs.

☐ Discuss and have insight into their own strengths and weaknesses.

☐ Improve communication with salon management and other staff.

☐ Have a goal of improved individual targets as well as team achievements.

☐ Agree on an action plan.

An accurate record of the meeting and your thoughts afterwards should be kept. It is very helpful if a pre-appraisal form is completed by the employee prior to the meeting, covering such topics as assessing their strengths and weaknesses, issues to be raised and requests for training. Examples of both appraisal forms are in Figures 5.6 (on pages 125–6) and 5.7 (on page 127).

Retaining staff

Finding good and suitable staff is not easy. Once you have gone through all the procedures of advertising, interviewing, selecting and training, you need to make sure that you don't easily lose them. Unfortunately, staff turnover in the beauty industry is very high. This could be due to:

☐ The average age of the therapists.

☐ The hard work.

☐ Boredom as they discover that being a beauty therapist is not quite what they thought it would be.

☐ The way they are treated.

☐ The generally low wages.

It is very difficult to overcome most of these factors. However, there are several steps you can take to minimise this problem and hopefully keep your good members of staff. Here are some suggestions:

CONFIDENTIAL

Name: _____

Job Title: _____

Date started: _____

The purpose of this appraisal is to help strengthen skills, improve performance, and plan appropriate individual training and development in a way that is compatible with personal interests and the interest of this company.

Please complete all questions giving thought and attention to them and expressing your honest feelings.

1. How closely do you feel your job description reflects the main duties and responsibilities that are given to you? _____

_____

2. What part of your job do you enjoy most? _____

_____

3. What part of your job or duties do you dislike most? _____

_____

4. Do you feel that your skills and abilities are being properly utilised in your job and duties? _____

_____

5. Are there any factors that are hindering your work or performance? If yes, please explain: _____

_____

6. On a scale of 1 to 10 (1 the lowest and 10 the highest), how happy are you with your

• Job _____

• Wages _____

• Hours of work _____

• Other members of staff _____

• Your manager _____

• Other (please specify) _____

7. To improve your job performance, what can be done by the following to assist you?

• Your manager _____

_____

• Yourself _____

_____

◀

● Anyone else _____

_____

8. Is there any area of your work for which you feel you need more training? _____

_____

9. What are your objectives and aims in your job and responsibilities? _____

_____

10. Please state anything else that you would like to be changed/considered in your job.

Signed: _____

Date: _____

Figure 5.6 Staff pre-appraisal questionnaire

☐ Make your salon a happy and friendly place; beauty salons have no room for moody, miserable and unsociable therapists. Avoid them or they will affect others.

☐ Make your staff feel good by encouraging them to achieve targets and then rewarding them.

☐ Give good incentives and make sure you act on them.

☐ Conduct happy and positive staff meetings, light and relaxed with some food and drink.

☐ Avoid the routine of 'therapist comes in . . . therapist works . . . therapist goes home'.

☐ Keep your staff motivated by regular training and getting them involved in various aspects of the salon.

☐ Have high respect for your staff and make sure others do as well.

☐ Be friendly with your staff, but firm and decisive. Don't let them think you are a softy and don't let them take you for granted.

☐ Treat them well; don't look down on them.

☐ Pay them well and what they are worth.

Performance criteria	Grade A high	B	C	D	E low
Dealing with customers					
Customer care					
Speed of work					
Quality of work					
Cleanliness					
Knowledge of products					
Knowledge of services					
Knowledge of prices and offers					
Ability to work in a team					
Initiative					
Motivation					
Attitude towards other members of staff					
General attitude					
Punctuality and timekeeping					
Maintenance of Health & Safety requirements					
Confidentiality					
Flexibility					
Appearance					

Name of staff member _____

Name of manager/owner _____ Date _____

Figure 5.7 Appraisal form

Disciplinary and grievance procedure

Even in the best-run businesses it may be necessary to take disciplinary action with staff. It is vital to have clear policies and procedures in place from the outset so as to treat all staff fairly and reasonably when problems occur. You should ensure that everyone is aware of the minimum standards of conduct required of them and what will happen if these standards are not met. All staff members should be aware of what happens in the event of disciplinary action being taken and their right of appeal, as well as their right to express a grievance in any matter relating to their employment with you.

Your disciplinary rules should be in writing and cover conduct issues including the following:

☐ Absence from work.

☐ Performance and standard of work.

☐ Bullying or harassment of colleagues.

☐ Persistent lateness for work and poor timekeeping.

☐ Lack of personal hygiene and poor personal appearance.

☐ Unauthorised use of the company's phone or internet for personal reasons during working hours (e.g. Facebook or personal e-mails).

☐ Unauthorised use of the company's products and equipment for personal benefit.

☐ Obtaining client details and doing treatments on company clients outside of work.

☐ Abuse of the confidentiality rules of the company.

☐ Smoking, or alcohol or drug consumption.

 This list is not exhaustive and there will be other disciplinary issues that you will need to add in relation to the unique needs and requirements of your own salon.

You will also need to give examples of gross misconduct, which is misconduct so serious as to pose a threat to continued employment with you. These could include:

☐ Theft or dishonesty.

☐ Causing harm to a client through gross negligence.

☐ Wilful damage to property and salon premises and equipment.

☐ Serious breaches of health and safety regulations and procedures.

☐ Drunkenness or drug abuse at work.

☐ Breaking the confidentiality rules.

DISCIPLINARY PROCEDURE

If a member of staff is failing to reach the standards of conduct or performance that is required of them, the first step should be an informal discussion. Talk to the person directly, explain the problem, listen to their reply and agree a plan of action together. Always try to give guidance and support to help your member of staff improve. If this does not resolve the issue a more formal approach may be required, such as:

1. A verbal warning.

2. A first written warning.

3. Following a disciplinary meeting, a second or final written warning stating the consequences for failure to improve.

4. Dismissal, only if the offence merits this action.

The statutory requirements and obligations for an employer are constantly changing and vary according the size of the business. On 6 April 2009 the Employment Act 2008 came into force which repealed the previous statutory dismissal, disciplinary and grievance procedures set out in the Employment Act 2002.

 Professional legal advice should always be sought to make sure that you are handling the disciplinary and grievance procedures correctly according to current legislation.

The basic principles to remember in handling any disciplinary or grievance issues are:

☐ Investigate the problem thoroughly before taking any action.

☐ Invite the employee to a meeting to discuss the issues. They have the right to be accompanied by either a work colleague or another person of their choice at the meeting.

☐ State the facts objectively to the employee.

☐ Listen to the employee's response.

☐ Consider any mitigating factors such as provocation or health issues, length of service and previous conduct and work record.

☐ Be fair and reasonable at all times.

☐ Be supportive of the employee by arranging additional training or mentoring if necessary.

☐ Tell the employee they have the right of appeal against the grievance procedure, should they wish to take matters further.

☐ Record all communications, formal and informal, in writing. Record any action to be taken and implement it as soon as possible.

 Always try to keep the lines of communication open with staff and try to resolve problems informally at an early stage if possible.

DISMISSAL

Staff may be dismissed at the end of a short-term or fixed-term contract or due to redundancy if there is a reduced need for staff within the business. Sometimes performance of individual members of staff may deteriorate, or changes in the economy and your business may dictate a need for the reduction of staff. Despite taking great care in trying to find the right people for the position in your salon, sometimes things don't work out due to poor performance, misconduct, substandard work or even a clash of personality.

In any event, make sure that all disciplinary and grievance procedures are properly carried out and the member of staff in question is given the opportunity to change before the ultimate sanction of dismissal is considered.

In the case of a dismissal, it is vitally important that as an employer:

- ☐ You give sufficient reason for dismissal.

- ☐ You have acted fairly and reasonably.

- ☐ You have followed all the correct procedures.

- ☐ You have been non-discriminatory.

Insurance companies and professional organisations such as BABTAC or The Guild of Beauty Therapists often provide advice lines for employment queries. In addition, some insurance companies will insure you to provide cover in cases of employment disputes, employment tribunals and compensation awards. In an increasingly litigious world, this is money well spent.

6
CLIENTS AND TREATMENTS

The lifeblood of your business is your customers and clients; without them flowing into and through your salon, you will have no business. It is therefore imperative that your salon attracts plenty of clients who will come back again and again. It is also imperative that the numbers grow steadily.

Dealing with customers and clients

A client or customer is a person or organisation that comes to you for a product, treatment or service. Generally speaking, a client receives a service or treatment, while a customer purchases a product. (For example, we are customers of Tesco, but clients of our dentists.) Most people don't distinguish between the terms and use one or the other, as it does not really matter.

The financial success of your beauty business will depend on the number of clients treated every day and the amount of products you sell. As there are only a certain number of hours in the day and only a fixed number of rooms in your salon, the only way of maximising your business turnover is by utilising the time available to you and your therapists as efficiently as possible and by selling as many products as possible.

Booking clients

Most salons work a nine-hour day, six days a week. That is a total of 54 working hours available each week. On average, there are always a lot of 10 minutes here, 15 minutes there between appointments. Taking into account the usual late arrivals, this adds up to an average of about 13 hours of each therapist's time each week. Taking into account that each therapist works, say, 40 hours per week, that is a staggering 32.5% or one-third of valuable time lost.

Such inefficiency is totally unacceptable in a business and must be avoided if the business is to prosper. It is vitally important, whenever possible, that for every minute of the day every available therapist is used to their maximum efficiency.

By implementing back-to-back bookings the salon will become much more profitable as all available appointment times will be fully utilised.

BACK-TO-BACK BOOKING

Avoid gaps of 10 minutes or 15 minutes between clients' appointments. When one treatment is finished, the therapist, while talking to the client, should start cleaning and tidying the treatment room and preparing it for the next client.

Arrange to do two treatments in the same treatment time whenever possible. For example, during a facial while a mask is on, you can do a leg wax or a re-varnish.

Remember to involve all members of staff. They can quite often come up with some good time-saving suggestions.

Don't forget the most important person involved is your receptionist, who can fill the odd 15 minute free slot with mini-treatments and ensure that the therapist's time is well used and optimised.

Gaining and retaining clients

Every business must grow and expand in order to prosper. As the costs of materials increase, wages go up, and rent rates and bills always go upwards, your salon's takings and profit must also increase accordingly. This can only be achieved by:

☐ Continuously improving the efficiency of your business.

☐ Reducing costs wherever possible.

☐ Increasing the number of customers and clients.

☐ Increasing the amount of products sold.

The following list makes some interesting points about retaining existing and gaining new clients and customers:

☐ It is essential not only to attract new customers but also to retain existing clients.

☐ It costs more to gain a new customer than to keep an old one.

☐ Most customers don't complain about a problem, they just don't come back.

☐ Because most customers don't complain, management is often lulled into thinking that all is well.

☐ On average one dissatisfied customer is likely to tell ten others who will in turn pass on the negative feedback about your salon.

☐ The average beauty salon in the UK loses about 30% of its existing clientèle each year, mostly because of either poor service or substandard treatments. Most of these clients could be retained.

☐ Salons offering good-quality treatments and customer care can charge 20% more for their services and grow twice as fast as their competitors.

☐ Regardless of the size of your salon, the link between excellent standards and service and profit is undeniable.

☐ Every time a satisfied customer leaves your salon with a good experience, they will help to generate at least five extra customers.

☐ Word of mouth is without doubt the best and most effective form of advertising for your salon. Make sure the experience is a good one for every client.

 Carry out a confidential customer satisfaction survey every six months to find out what is really going on with your business.

Conducting a client survey

A confidential survey will give you valuable in-depth information about what your customers and clients really think and feel about your salon. Their feedback should be analysed and, after consultation with your staff and therapists, any necessary action taken. This is probably the most effective way of learning how to improve

At **XXXX Beauty Salon** we aim to achieve a high standard of treatment while keeping our customers fully satisfied with all aspects of their treatments and our salon.

In order to maintain and continuously improve the standard of our services, we need to know about the experience you have had at our salon.

Please complete this questionnaire and hand it to one of our staff. All responses will be treated in the strictest confidence.

PLEASE CIRCLE ONE NUMBER TO INDICATE HOW SATISFIED YOU ARE

10 Extremely satisfied
1 Totally dissatisfied

Contacting us:	1 2 3 4 5 6 7 8 9 10
Making the appointment:	1 2 3 4 5 6 7 8 9 10
The receptionist:	1 2 3 4 5 6 7 8 9 10
The appointment time you requested:	1 2 3 4 5 6 7 8 9 10
Waiting before your treatment started:	1 2 3 4 5 6 7 8 9 10
Your treatment:	1 2 3 4 5 6 7 8 9 10
The therapist:	1 2 3 4 5 6 7 8 9 10
Post-treatment:	1 2 3 4 5 6 7 8 9 10
Billing and payment procedure:	1 2 3 4 5 6 7 8 9 10
Standard of cleanliness and hygiene:	1 2 3 4 5 6 7 8 9 10
Product purchase:	1 2 3 4 5 6 7 8 9 10
Information and explanations given by staff:	1 2 3 4 5 6 7 8 9 10
Salon atmosphere:	1 2 3 4 5 6 7 8 9 10

Based on your own experience, would you recommend
XXXX Beauty Salon to a friend or family?   1 2 3 4 5 6 7 8 9 10

How often do you visit us?   1/week   1/month   2/month   Irregularly

Any other comments or suggestions you wish to add _____

_____

_____

Thank you for your time.

Figure 6.1 Client survey questionnaire

your service. A sample of a typical questionnaire is shown in Figure 6.1. You can always change the questions and add ones that are appropriate to your salon and staff.

You could offer a prize draw for all entries to encourage participation. Good ideas for prizes are a free treatment, a gift voucher or a product. Have a neat box in the reception area where all completed forms can be left.

A client survey is also an excellent way of collecting customers' e-mail addresses for future marketing and promotions.

 Contacting customers by e-mail is a cost-effective way of keeping in touch by offering promotions. A quarterly newsletter, for example, reminds clients of what you have on offer and makes them feel valued.

DEALING WITH NEGATIVE FEEDBACK AND COMPLAINTS

If your customer questionnaires reveal any negative comments, and those comments are not made anonymously, you could contact the customer either by e-mail or with a phone call to discuss the problem. If the issue is serious, it may be necessary to invite the client in for a one-to-one meeting. No one likes criticism and as therapists we are more used to hearing positive comments about our treatments, so it is not easy to receive negative feedback and complaints, especially those without foundation, but we must be able to deal with these situations calmly and professionally.

Sometimes the first sign of a dissatisfied customer is their failure to turn up for a subsequent pre-booked appointment without explanation.

 Always keep a record of all no-shows on each client's treatment or attendance card and contact them regarding their missed appointment.

More commonly, the complainant will contact the salon by phone or by letter stating their dissatisfaction with the treatment. At the same time, it is quite usual for the complainant to request a refund for one of the following reasons:

☐ The treatment has not worked.

☐ The treatment did not meet the client's expectations.

☐ The treatment has caused harm or injury in some way.

When an official complaint has been received, it must be recorded according to the salon's policy and procedure for complaints and, if it is an injury which may result in a claim, the insurance company should be notified immediately.

 Make sure that your salon has a policy and procedure for handling complaints and that everyone who works in the salon is aware of it and knows what to do.

One of the simplest ways of recording all your complaints (hopefully there are not many) is to have a complaint book designated for this purpose, kept in a convenient place at the reception. The book should be lined and have columns for the date of the treatment, client name, address, telephone number, e-mail address and nature of the complaint, the date the complaint was reported and any comments made by the client. Also make a note of any preferred time for the manager to call to discuss the problem.

 While taking a complaint (by telephone or in person), listen carefully, take notes and sympathetically apologise, but *do not* admit liability. If you do, it could adversely affect your insurance policy on renewal.

Receiving injury claims

We talked about clients' record cards in Chapter 3. If you receive an injury complaint which involves a claim, these cards are vitally important and are needed by your insurance company. They are your main source of defence and the only documented evidence of events. It is most important that you always make sure every client has filled in a client card prior to treatment or you might not be covered by your insurance policy in the event of a claim. These client record cards need to be kept securely for six years with confidentiality and data protection issues being taken into account. Under the statute of limitations, claims for injury can be brought against you for up to three years after the event and, in some instances, such as clients under 18 years of age, this time limit may be extended.

Client cards should be clean and clearly readable, and any alterations or crossings out should be initialled and dated. Make notes of any advice, price quotations, leaflets or verbal information that was given to the client prior to or during the treatments. It is important that any unusual reactions or incidents are recorded at the time, as well as any post-treatment advice. This information will be used by your insurers in the event of a major claim.

If a complaint or claim is made, do not immediately offer a refund. Offering a refund for a treatment could be misconstrued as admitting liability for the damage or injury. If the complaint is serious or potentially serious, it should be immediately reported to your insurance company. They will send you a disclaimer which states that by offering the refund you do not accept liability for any loss or damage now or in the future. The client should sign this before accepting any refund.

Here is a summary of what to do in case of a complaint against your salon or a claim for a treatment.

☐ Listen carefully and write down everything the client says, not forgetting the time, date and the client's full details.

☐ Ask as many relevant questions as possible, and record all the replies.

☐ Be sympathetic and apologetic, but do not make any comments that might have an adverse effect later.

☐ Do not accept blame or liability and do not immediately offer a refund.

☐ Give any relevant advice that may help the damage or injury and prevent further damage where possible.

☐ Apologise and try to find out what the client wants.

☐ Sometimes the complainant just wants a correction to treatment, or a subsequent free treatment. If so, having established that there is no injury and no claim, ask them if they will be happy with such an offer and accept it with your compliments.

☐ If there is an injury (small or serious) or a claim, apologise and reassure the client that you will be in touch as soon as possible.

☐ Contact your insurance company and follow their advice.

☐ Make sure that everything you or your staff do and say is recorded in writing.

☐ Keep your staff well informed about all complaints and claims so that they learn from the experience.

Most insurers offer a 24-hour legal advice helpline which you can use. But make sure that you contact them promptly as some policies have a 30-day deadline for any incident, to remain covered.

We are all human and we all make mistakes. Prolonged self-doubt can be corrosive and damaging to you and your business. It is important to learn from all complaints and talk them through with your staff no matter how minor they are. This way you can prevent incidents recurring and improve the quality of your treatments and services.

How to avoid complaints

Most complaints are normally minor – being kept waiting too long, or missing a patch when waxing, are the most common – and are easily resolved. But if your instinct tells you that the complaint may escalate, always get help and advice before proceeding.

The following is a list of suggestions which will help avoid complaints and treatment accidents:

☐ The most obvious solution for avoiding complaints is to have well-trained staff with a **professional attitude** and **good customer care**. Customer care and the standards required of your staff in your salon must be reinforced at every opportunity. Have training sessions, role play involving different scenarios and discussions during your staff meetings on the best way of handling different situations.

☐ Staff must know the **contra-indications** for all your treatments. They should not hesitate to ask the manager for advice when they are in doubt about whether a particular treatment should be performed or recommended. One very common problem is waxing on the face, such as eyebrows, when the client is on roacutane or using products containing AHAs or retinol. This question is easily overlooked during a busy day but if you fail to check, the result can be a burn as these

139

products are contra-indicated and make the client much more susceptible to an adverse reaction.

☐ Make sure all customers receive a **patch test** for tinting, peels or where allergies have been raised as an issue. When a client makes a booking for an eyelash tint, make sure that a test patch has been done 24 hours before their first treatment at your salon, even if they have had tints done before elsewhere. The treatment might have been done with another brand and it is vital that you cover yourself in the rare case of an allergic reaction.

☐ Make sure that your equipment is well maintained, kept clean and serviced according to the manufacturer's instructions. Keep complete records of all breakdowns, repairs and servicing that the therapy equipment has and ensure that the staff using the equipment are adequately trained.

☐ Under the Electricity at Work Act 1989 you have a responsibility to have all electrical appliances tested annually by a qualified electrical engineer.

☐ Another important piece of legislation to consider is the Workplace (health, safety and welfare) Regulations 1992, which ensure that the workplace is a safe and healthy place for employees and customers. These regulations relate to every part of your business premises, from the reception and treatment rooms to the stairs and passageways. At all times make sure there are no tripping hazards or slippery surfaces, especially on the stairs. For more information on your obligations under the current legislation, see Chapters 2 and 3.

☐ You will find that most complaints seem to flow from misunderstandings or communication breakdowns. To avoid these, try to establish a good rapport with your clients and build up a good therapeutic business/customer relationship. Avoid overselling treatments and products with false promises of results that can't be achieved; be realistic with the likely result and outcome. Know when to refer when appropriate, particularly if a condition or situation is beyond the scope of what you have been trained to do, or where you feel you are out of your depth, or you feel uncertain of the client.

☐ Before the treatment commences, the therapist should get confirmation from the client of exactly what treatments they require. This avoids misunderstandings and mistakes made in the bookings and allows the therapist to manage the treatment time more effectively.

☐ At the end of the treatment the therapist should ask the client to check the result, using a hand mirror if necessary, and whether they are happy with their treatment. The receptionist should also enquire, 'Was everything alright with your treatment today?'

Client care

Gaining customers and clients is hard enough, but retaining them requires a lot of care and attention. Your customers and clients need to be looked after and this involves more than a good treatment. Here we discuss various ways of keeping your clients and customers loyal to your business.

ON ARRIVAL

When the client arrives at your salon they should be shown to the waiting room and asked, if it is their first visit, to fill in a client record card. The receptionist should notify the therapist of the client's arrival and the therapist should then go and introduce herself to the client and take them to the treatment room. The therapist should always try to be on time as this is part of being a complete professional. The client's record card and contra-indications to treatment must be reviewed prior to every treatment, even with regulars, to ensure that the treatment is safe and appropriate.

COMMUNICATING WITH YOUR CLIENT

Relating well to other people is an essential part of being a beauty therapist. Clients who return time and time again to your salon are the very core of your business and the secret of keeping them happy is by making every customer feel special and understood, empathising with their concerns and providing expert advice and solutions to their needs.

Some important points to remember are:

☐ Greet the client by name and introduce yourself.

☐ Maintain eye contact.

☐ Smile, don't be serious and miserable.

☐ When the treatment allows, sit facing the client, leaning forward slightly.

☐ Nod appropriately.

☐ Do not hold conversations with other staff or on your mobile phone when with your client – focus on your customer.

Asking questions is one of the best ways to get to know clients and their needs. But to communicate effectively you need to ask questions which are relevant, not personal and in the right way. There are two kinds of question:

1. Open: these questions can't be answered with a 'yes' or a 'no'. They invite the client to express themselves, their concerns and reveal a little more detail. They make the client feel valued. They are useful in defusing heated discussions or complaints as the client will feel that their opinion is being heard.

2. Closed: these are direct questions and should be used when you need a quick reply, normally a 'yes' or a 'no' or some facts.

Part of being a good communicator is being comfortable with silence. It is just as important to know when to be quiet as it is to be able to talk. This is a key skill to develop during your career, knowing when to make small talk and when to allow the client to relax in peace.

 Remember that the client is paying for your time and it is they who should lead the way on whether to chatter or not.

Try not to talk about yourself but concentrate on your client – not everyone wants to know the ups and downs of your love life.

 Do not risk offending your client by asking personal questions or discussing controversial topics as this can make your client feel uncomfortable if their views differ from yours.

But the words that we say are only a part of our communication skills. Non-verbal communication such as body language is just as important in how we come across and our perception of others. A good therapist should be able to pick up non-verbal signals if the client is feeling anxious or uncomfortable during a treatment, and then respond appropriately.

The usual warning signals include:

☐ Fidgeting, tension or stiffness in the body.

☐ Frowning during a treatment.

☐ Gripping the table or couch.

Do not plough on regardless, but sensitively ask the client if everything is alright. Take a few minutes out from the treatment to explain what you are doing and if necessary lighten your touch or make the client more comfortable. They often open up and talk.

Make sure that you are relaxed and comfortable and feel positive with the client and in what you are doing. This will be reflected in your own body language, which will be picked up by the client. This area of communication is also discussed in Chapter 11.

BE A GOOD LISTENER

The most essential communication skill is the ability to listen. Being a good listener helps trust to develop between the therapist and client and helps you both get the best out of a treatment. As a therapist, you can pick up so much information simply by listening to what your client wants and expects from the treatment. The client in turn will feel valued and cared for and will be more likely to follow any recommendations that you may make.

MAKE YOUR CLIENT FEEL GOOD

Apart from being a good listener and communicating well, there are other important things that you can do:

☐ Make your client feel that you are happy to treat them.

☐ Stay focused on your client at all times – that is what they expect.

☐ Concentrate on what the client is saying to you and show interest by either responding appropriately, including nodding and/or by asking another question.

☐ Keep eye contact and smile.

☐ Encourage your clients to express their concerns and needs by asking them open questions and listening to their replies.

☐ Affirm your client's feelings and needs by paraphrasing them and repeating them. This will reassure them that you have been listening and have understood and empathised.

☐ Allow your client the time and space to open up by letting them lead the conversation at their pace.

☐ Be comfortable with silence if the client wants to relax.

☐ Be non-judgmental.

☐ Be sensitive to non-verbal body language, and respond accordingly if possible.

☐ Try to remember things that the client has told you on previous visits. Write brief notes on client record cards if necessary to remind yourself or other staff.

☐ Never discuss your client's confidential conversation with anyone else.

Client record cards

A client record card should be filled in by every client prior to treatment. This is not only a legal requirement for your insurance but also is an invaluable record for the therapist and salon manager. Keeping complete records has become much less time-consuming since the advent of computerised records, but if you keep your records on computer be aware of your legal obligations under the Data Protection Act 1998. This requires you to keep all data securely protected and you may also have to notify the Information Commissioner that you are storing this data. A good source of information is www.ico.gov.uk

Written client record cards should be filed alphabetically and kept in a secure lockable cabinet and treated with strict confidentiality. A full record should provide the following information:

☐ Contact details for the client including address, home or work telephone numbers, mobile number and e-mail address. Highlight the preferred method of contact and note if marketing material or special offers can be sent either by post or e-mail.

☐ Date of birth. This can be used for special promotions such as sending a birthday card linked to a promotion, for example, for a free manicure with a facial.

☐ Medical history which could reveal any contra-indications to treatment.

☐ Treatment history showing what treatments were carried out, by whom, how much was charged, which treatments were recommended and the price quoted.

☐ Note should be made of any reaction to treatment, especially adverse reactions such as excessive erythema or bruising. A record should also be made of any advice given such as avoiding the sun or applying an antiseptic cream post-treatment. This could prove vital if any complaint is received.

☐ Facial treatments should be very clearly documented to show skin analysis, which products were used in case of an allergic reaction, whether extraction was done and if high frequency or galvanic current was used. In times of staff illness or changes, this will provide an accurate record for consistent treatment by the next therapist. This will ensure client loyalty and could avoid the loss of a valued customer.

☐ A record of any product sales will act as a reminder to check how the client is finding using the product and if they need any replacements or additional products. If samples have been given, always follow up with the client to see if they have any feedback. Remembering these details can make the client feel special and make the difference to making a sale or not.

☐ Record the progress achieved and any problems encountered on the way. Photos before and after treatment are an accurate way of recording this and can clearly illustrate to the client how far they have progressed during the treatment plan.

☐ Client records also act as a check against financial accounts, staff commissions and to document treatments completed within a treatment course.

The Data Protection Act

When collecting and storing personal information on clients and employees, you need to be aware of the Data Protection Act 1998. This Act applies to both written and computer-held information or data, and requires the business owner to comply with the following points:

☐ Safely and securely store all data to ensure confidentiality.

☐ Allow access to this data if requested by the individual concerned.

☐ Store only data that is necessary.

☐ Stored information must be adequate, relevant and not excessive for the nature of the business.

In some circumstances you may need to register with the Information Commissioner. The rules concerning this can be complex and most beauty salons will be exempt. However, it is advisable to check, as failure to do so, if required, is a criminal offence. Check online at www.businesslink.gov.uk or phone the Information Commissioner's Office Data Protection helpline on 0845 630 60 60.

Client consultation

A client consultation is invaluable for the salon owner to find out what the client's needs and beauty concerns are and to find a solution and recommend treatments and products. It is highly recommended that you provide free consultations with clients and always prior to a face or body treatment. However, sometimes informal consultations can be done during a manicure, pedicure or even waxing treatments. There is a number of objectives of a client consultation.

- ☐ It provides a welcome and an introduction to your salon.

- ☐ You can listen to clients as they explain their concerns and needs. It is important to communicate with your client, empathise and listen to what they say. Ask direct questions which require direct replies, such as 'Are you currently on any medication?'; and open questions to discover more about your client, such as 'Tell me about your concerns regarding your skin'.

- ☐ You can establish a rapport and the client's trust in you as a therapist and in your specialist knowledge.

- ☐ It forms a baseline assessment and evaluation of the problem and if there are any contra-indications to treatment.

- ☐ It provides an opportunity for you to demonstrate your professional expertise by offering a solution to the client's concerns. There are many reasons why clients seek advice from a beauty salon. It may be a weight or skin problem, a wish for improvement or a desire for a new image, but all require a solution which the salon should provide.

- ☐ You get the opportunity to explain what treatments are available in language that the client understands, dispelling any anxieties that the client may have.

- ☐ You can design an individual treatment plan, explaining what that entails, including potential side-effects, the cost implications and the likely outcome.

It is important to give a balanced and honest view and recommendations. If you overstate the likely outcome, it will only result in a disappointed and dissatisfied customer.

Consultations should be carried out in a quiet and private area of the salon to ensure confidentiality. With tactful questioning and a non-judgmental, reassuring manner a skilled therapist should instil a sense of confidence in the client, who must feel that their problems have been understood and that they have a good chance of being resolved with treatment. A successful consultation will result in a treatment being booked, and a happy client with realistic expectations of the outcome and the time scale, as well as the financial commitments involved.

 Never be pushy. Listen to the client and be sincere in your suggestions or recommendations. Emphasise the benefits of the recommended treatment or product and give the best advice you can – your clients will recognise this and come to trust you.

Treatments

The treatments and services that you offer in your salon will depend on which product range you choose. Many skincare companies have both body and facial treatments, each with its own technique and method. The companies will provide training for your staff along with a manual to refer to.

 When choosing what services to offer in your salon, don't forget who your market is. The treatments must appeal to your clients and not just to you. If your clients are mature, their interest will tend to lie more with anti-ageing treatments. On the other hand, if your salon has a younger clientèle, then spray tanning or Brazilian waxing would be more popular. Another factor to consider is how affluent your locality is – a £150 treatment may sell well in the heart of London's Knightsbridge but not necessarily elsewhere.

Preparing for treatments

Clients put their trust in you as a beauty professional. You are there to offer expert advice and treatments, so you must 'look the part'. It is important to maintain the highest standards of professionalism in all aspects of your working life and to remember that the client/therapist relationship is based on trust, empathy and mutual respect.

STANDARDISE TREATMENTS

It is most important to have consistency in all the treatments offered in your salon. Clients expect to receive every treatment the same way and with the same procedure, no matter when they come and who does the treatment.

Obviously every therapist has been trained differently and is often accustomed to doing things in a different way and may have a different routine. In order to achieve consistency in treatments, produce a list of procedures and make sure everyone follows the routine step by step. As an example, a treatment routine for a deluxe pedicure is given in Figure 6.2.

UNIFORMS

It is important to present yourself in a professional manner so that the client has confidence in you. All members of staff should wear a matching uniform. Although most salons provide uniforms for staff, some salons require employees to buy and supply their own. There are several companies supplying uniforms to the health and beauty industry, and attending the trade exhibitions is a great way to see what is available. Keep your salon theme in mind when choosing uniforms.

Your uniform needs to be:

☐ Cool in summer.

☐ Warm in winter (maybe by allowing staff to wear a plain cardigan in a matching colour to the uniform).

☐ Loose-fitting enough to allow freedom of movement.

☐ Practical.

☐ Easy to wash, ideally with no or minimal ironing required.

☐ Appropriate and professional.

1. Ask client to pick a colour

2. Sit them down and get them to soak feet in the foot spa

3. Cut and file right foot

4. Apply cuticle remover and soak foot

5. Cut and file left foot

6. Apply cuticle remover and soak foot

7. Push back cuticles on right foot and clip if needed

8. Scrub and soak right foot

9. Push back cuticles on left foot and clip if needed

10. Scrub and soak left foot

11. Rasp dead skin off right foot

12. Buff nails – apply cuticle oil

13. Massage

14. Apply paraffin wax, put foot in plastic bag/cling wrap, then in mitts

15. Repeat steps 11–14 on left foot

16. Use polish remover to remove any excess oil or cream

17. Apply base coat

18. Apply two coats of polish

19. Apply top coat

20. Spray with quick dry

21. If possible, ask client to wait 5-10 minutes for it to dry before they leave

Figure 6.2 Treatment routine for a deluxe pedicure – 75 minutes

Comfortable shoes or sandals are essential as therapists are on their feet most of the day. Ideally staff should have matching colours and styles in footwear – no Doc Martins or flamboyant Day-Glo trainers.

TREATMENT ROOM

The treatment room should be welcoming, warm, clean and comfortable. The couch should be prepared for the clients, before their arrival, with all products and equipment ready for use. Clean couch roll should be on the bed, together with towels and a robe. A pleasant aroma such as lavender or citrus is lovely for the client to experience when entering the room.

Treat all the senses with mood lighting, clean fluffy towels, nice smells, and relaxing music playing in the background.

 Don't forget your customer's preferences when choosing music. Aim for music that is not too loud or intrusive and not too unconventional in style. Drum and bass or hip hop may not be the choice of all your customers.

 For customers who have limited time, consider having two therapists doing two treatments at the same time. For example, giving a facial while a manicure is being done. Or do an eyelash tint or shape and paint while the mask is on.

Facial treatments

In addition to the usual range of facials offered by your skincare company, there are several additional treatments that you could introduce to keep your clients interested and eager to try. The trade exhibitions are a great source of ideas such as:

- □ Vitamin C facial

- □ Micro-dermabrasion

- □ Skin peels

- □ Chocolate facial

 Try not to be gimmicky but look for treatments that will appeal to the client and produce results.

Skin peels

Similar results to micro-dermabrasion can be achieved with the application of skin peels, which give a deep exfoliating effect. Peels can be used to treat ageing, sun damage, scarring and acne. There are several types of peel on the market, the best known being Skinceuticals and MD Formulations.

The major plus points of peels include the following:

☐ They are quick and easy to use, giving good results.

☐ The peels can be adapted to suit all skin types, giving a milder or stronger peel as required.

☐ As no machine is required there is no large initial outlay and treatment costs are low, giving an excellent return on your investment.

☐ They are an excellent alternative to micro-dermabrasion.

The average cost of the product (50 treatments) is £60 to £200.

Eyelash extensions

Professionally-applied semi-permanent eyelash extensions are the hottest new treatment on offer in salons at the moment. The false eyelashes are individually glued onto the existing eyelash, making it fuller, longer and more visible. The results can last for up to 12 weeks.

There are several companies offering start-up packages including training and promotional material at a cost of £300 to £1,000.

Some of the plus points of this treatment are:

☐ Training usually takes one day, with practice back at the salon.

☐ Due to the popularity of this treatment many salons are charging between £50 and £150 for a set.

☐ Due to high demand at present, the treatment gives an excellent return on your original investment.

The main drawbacks are:

☐ After the training, the therapist needs a lot of practice.

□ Applying the eyelashes requires precision, skill and patience and can take up to an hour.

Cosmetic procedures

It is becoming increasingly common to find beauty salons offering cosmetic procedures such as Botox, dermal fillers and tooth whitening. There are many companies and individuals who will come to your salon on a regular basis to carry out these treatments. This benefits the doctor or dentist who picks up new clients for cosmetic procedures from your business and also benefits your salon by enabling you to offer a premium service to your clients with minimum outlay or investment.

If you decide to use any of these services, be aware of the following:

□ Currently only qualified medical experts are allowed to administer dermal fillers or Botox.

□ Tooth whitening must be carried out by a qualified dentist. Although there are several companies heavily promoting this service to salons for therapists to perform, the chemicals used to whiten the teeth can damage gums and cause chemical burns if applied incorrectly.

□ Make sure your doctor or dentist is fully qualified and insured. Obtain photocopies of their qualifications and insurance policies for your business records before you make any agreement.

The cost of these treatments is minimal and usually on a profit-share basis.

 If you have the space available, this is an excellent low-cost and low-risk way to offer cosmetic procedures to your clients. Consistent client demand is there and these treatments are likely to remain popular.

Body treatments

The most popular body treatment service in your salon is likely to be waxing. To draw and keep clients to your salon for this very popular treatment, consider ways in which you can stand out from other local salons:

☐ Have spotlessly clean treatment rooms, floors and wax pots.

☐ Use top-quality wax.

☐ Offer the client a choice of waxes and professional advice on which is the best wax for them.

☐ Use experienced therapists who are quick and efficient in waxing skills.

☐ Offer specialist services such as Brazilians or pubic hair colouring.

☐ Offer exceptional customer service.

WARM OR STRIP WAX

This type of wax is made from a combination of wax, oils and resins and has a low melting point. It is spread thinly with a spatula and removed with a material or paper strip. There is a variety of brands on the market and it is worth trying several before choosing. Some are a cream-based formula for sensitive skin; others have additional ingredients such as lavender or tea tree oil which are chosen for their anti-bacterial and soothing properties.

An increasingly popular method of applying warm wax is with a roller which is stored in a heated container to maintain its correct temperature. The advantage of this method is that it is quick; however, rollers are more expensive than wax sold in pots.

The advantages of warm or strip wax:

☐ Disposable, which helps to prevent cross-infection between clients.

☐ Low cost and economical to use.

☐ Quick and easy to use and maintain.

☐ Low working temperature.

The disadvantages of warm or strip wax:

☐ Not as effective on strong and coarse hair.

HOT WAX

Hot wax has become more popular in recent years and is made from a mixture of wax and synthetic resins. Before the wax is applied, a thin layer of oil or talc is applied to the area, preventing the wax from sticking to the skin but allowing the hot wax to grip the hair. A thick layer of the hot wax is then applied with a spatula, allowed to set and then peeled off.

There are several makes of hot wax available, but the effectiveness, pliability and ease of use of each vary considerably. The new generations of hot waxes are far superior to the brittle beeswax of the past, and are led by the Australian waxes such as *Lycon*, *Adam and Eve* and *Australian Bodycare* which are far more flexible and easier to use than others. Unfortunately they are much more expensive but clients are increasingly demanding these high-quality waxes as the popularity of Brazilian waxing grows.

 The increased cost of the hot wax must be built into your higher treatment charge for these specialist services.

The advantages of hot wax:

☐ Very effective for strong hair.

☐ Less painful for sensitive areas.

The disadvantages of hot wax:

☐ More expensive than warm wax.

☐ Slower to use.

 As the demand for Brazilian and Hollywood waxing grows, there is a real opportunity for beauty salons to specialise in this technique using the new generation of hot waxes. Take a specialist training course for advanced waxing techniques and offer this service to your clients.

The wax heater should be thermostatically controlled to maintain the correct working temperature throughout the day. It should be easily cleanable, have an outer casing that is cool to the touch, and be earthed and correctly wired.

Another service to consider when doing Brazilian waxing is pubic hair dying, which is growing in popularity. One of the best-known makes, which has been on the market since 2007, is Betty Beauty. There are 10 colours available, ranging from black and blond to blue and hot pink. They are safe and easy to use. For further information, visit www.bettybeauty.co.uk or purchase from www.westonebeauty.co.uk

Costings for different waxes:

Strip wax per pot:	£3 to £15 (enough for 4 full legs)
Hot wax:	£6 to £20 per kilo (enough for 6 Brazilian waxes)
Each roller:	£6 to £10 (enough for 2 full legs)

Nail services

Manicures and pedicures are always a popular treatment with clients and there are several ways in which you can make your salon a bit different from others:

☐ Choose a high-quality range of nail products.

☐ Have a spotlessly clean working area. No nail clippings on the floor, please.

☐ Maintain the highest standards of hygiene and sterilisation. Make sure your client sees you clean the tools.

☐ Consider offering your client the opportunity to purchase their own nail file or tools for future visits. These could be kept in a folder for their exclusive use.

☐ Be quick and efficient, with all the necessary tools to hand.

☐ Employ only experienced nail technicians.

The choice of nail product is very much a matter of preference. Try various ranges at the trade shows and see what you prefer and what's hot in the beauty press. Among the best makes are *Essie*, *Toma*, *OPI* and *Jessica*.

Acrylic, fibreglass or gel nails

Artificial nails are very popular and an excellent addition to the beauty salon's treatment list. They:

☐ are inexpensive to get started with

☐ don't need any additional space

☐ are always popular with clients.

Acrylic or fibreglass nails are created by mixing powder with blue liquid and is applied with a thick tapered brush. It is strong and great for tips or extensions but it can damage the natural nail, especially when removed incorrectly. Acrylic also has a strong odour during its application so bear this in mind if you are in a basement or a smaller salon, where you will need good ventilation.

Gel nails look more natural and are less damaging to the natural nail. But they are definitely not as strong, especially if applying tips or extensions, and they are prone to lifting and discoloration. The gel is applied with a brush and cured under UV light. There is less dust and odour with their application than with acrylic nails.

 Artificial nail products are only as good as the technician who applies them. Make sure you start off with a good training course, practise your skills and keep improving your knowledge.

7
SELECTING PRODUCTS, EQUIPMENT AND FURNITURE

IN THIS CHAPTER

- ☐ Which products should I use?

- ☐ How should I buy the products?

- ☐ What equipment do I need?

- ☐ Should I buy a laser machine?

- ☐ Facial equipment

- ☐ Skincare equipment

- ☐ Body toning equipment

- ☐ Should I have sunbeds and spray tanning machines?

- ☐ Nail equipment

- ☐ Portable equipment

- ☐ Hiring and leasing equipment

This chapter explains the exciting process of filling your salon with stock and equipment. We will consider the various factors to be taken into account when choosing a skincare brand for your salon and also cover the choices available to you regarding the wide range of beauty therapy equipment. Your salon will be selling products as well as using them in treatments, and you will be looking for a brand which complements your salon's ethos as well as bringing in profit for you. As a salon owner, you should also be aware of certain legislation relevant to the business such as The Sale of Goods and Supply of Services Acts 1982, 1994 and 2002.

Products

SELECTING YOUR PRODUCT RANGE

This is the most exciting part of setting up your salon. Take your time and do your research. There are many companies out there all eager for your business. Look in the professional beauty magazines such as *Vitality*, *The Guild*, *Health and Beauty* or *Spa World* and you will see numerous adverts for product houses and lines. Other great sources of information are the professional beauty shows and exhibitions which are held throughout the year in London, Manchester, Birmingham and Scotland. And if you really want to find that something different, why not consider going to one of the International Beauty Exhibitions held throughout the world? The biggest and best is COSMOPROF which is held in Bologna, Italy in the spring and in Hong Kong in the autumn. Here you will be astonished at the choice of products, equipment and new treatments.

However, don't get carried away and don't let the excitement of these exhibitions cloud your business head. Ask yourself the following questions before you go into buying mode:

☐ Does the foreign manufacturer or distributor have a support system in the UK?

☐ What is the cost of shipping? Transporting heavy items to the UK could make the item prohibitively expensive.

☐ Would the treatment or product appeal to your market? Don't get carried away when you are buying and forget who your target market is and if the product will fit into your business brand.

☐ What are the tax implications? Goods imported into the UK are liable for import duties and VAT. Various taxes and fees and delivery charges could add as much as 30% to your cost price and make the item very expensive.

☐ Does the equipment have a CE kite mark? Without this you will not be able to get insurance to cover the use of the machine and will therefore not be able to use it in the UK. *This is vitally important for the use of equipment such as lasers.*

☐ Does the manufacturer or distributor offer training and technical support for the equipment? What happens if the machine breaks down? Does the manufacturer offer services and maintenance cover?

☐ How long has the equipment or product been on the market and has it been tested and proven?

Generally speaking, going to exhibitions abroad is extremely useful, fun and an eye opener. But purchasing abroad in the early days of your business is not recommended.

Remember to keep all your travel and accommodation receipts when you go to trade fairs here and abroad. If you are self employed all such costs are considered as legitimate business expenses and can be offset against your earnings.

What to look for in a product range

Selecting the correct range of products for use in the salon or for retail is extremely important. The following list of suggestions will help you decide:

☐ A product line whose branding and ethos is complementary to your own salon. It is no use having a high-tech anti-ageing brand full of powerful expensive chemical ingredients if your salon has a natural, organic vibe catering to a student market.

☐ A product that meets the needs of your business with regard to the range of treatments, their results and sales. Consider if you have the room or client demand to offer body treatments or do you just require a simple yet effective skincare brand?

☐ A product line that meets the needs and aspirations of your customers. Do your clients want expensive high-end products or are they more cost-conscious? Do they want a brand they know and recognise or would they be willing to take a risk with an unknown line?

☐ A product line that offers training and support for your business and grows with the market, offering new and relevant products. Companies have got to keep up to date with what is currently on the market and update their products on a regular basis. Ask what the company offers for your business. Free training and refresher courses really help in controlling costs when employing new staff. An allocated supply of free samples, leaflets and other promotional materials really supports your business and helps you sell products and services.

☐ A product with a USP (Unique Selling Point) or 'hot' eye-catching ingredient. All products have a selling lifespan. Demand grows, demand peaks and demand wanes. You should offer a product that your clients will queue and ask for. You need to be able to spot the rising hot product as the market demand rises, not when it's declining. Keep your ear to the ground, try to spot what's going to be hot and sometimes take a risk.

☐ A product line that offers your business the flexibility it needs. Most companies will require you to have a minimum opening order or even minimum-size reorders. Ask whether you must take on the whole range, which will involve a large financial investment and products that you don't want.

☐ A product range that makes you a profit.

How to choose a product range

Here are some suggestions which will make your choice of product range less risky:

☐ Investigate the market thoroughly before making your choice. There are so many companies offering vast ranges of products that the choice can be overwhelming.

☐ Read the trade magazines for articles and advertisements for the main suppliers. Some magazines highlight certain treatment areas or concerns each month and have a whole article comparing the products on the market. These are especially useful and can save a lot of time when you are doing your research.

☐ Go to the main beauty trade exhibitions where all the well-known companies will be showcasing their products and treatments.

☐ Visit various stands and after consultation request brochures and samples.

☐ Ask for demonstrations or try out a treatment.

☐ Keep in mind your clients and their needs and requirements.

☐ Ask questions of the representatives and make notes so that you can compare what they offer. The following are some useful questions you could ask:

   – Do they offer free training?

   – Is training unlimited as you add new staff or is there a cost in the future?

   – Where is the training centre and will training be available in your salon? Remember to factor in the cost of getting yourself and your staff to a training centre and the travelling or overnight accommodation costs that may be incurred.

– Do they offer free samples? If not, what is the cost? Samples are essential to successful sales – most clients want to try before they buy.

– Do they supply posters, brochures and other salon support materials? And what is the cost? Or do you receive a free allocation according to how much you order?

– Will the company help with marketing? Will you be featured on their website of approved stockists?

– Does the company have a policy of restricting who stocks the range in a specific area? This will limit competition for a particular range if you can gain exclusivity in your area.

– Do you have the support of a business development consultant from the company? They normally visit monthly or bi-monthly and a good consultant can be a valuable asset to your business. They will keep you updated on any new additions to the range, offer sales and marketing advice and offer support.

– Will they help and support promotional events? A launch day/evening can really help get your new range off to a flying start and generate new client leads.

– Will the company help with advertising?

 Don't forget what you are looking for in a range for your salon. Write the key points down and compare them with the main selling points in the product ranges that are offered by your shortlisted companies.

Opening orders

Having been to several trade shows and exhibitions, looked through trade magazines and spoken to various suppliers, now is the time to choose a range of products that will be used in your salon.

Most skincare companies require you to purchase an opening minimum order in order to take on their products. There is often an added incentive to take on this launch offer of a free tester unit, free training or a discount off the normal package price. But beware, you may have to buy everything that they suggest, even the slow-selling products in the range, the ones that you don't really want and which you could be left with as unsellable stock.

 Try to negotiate the cost and what is included in the opening order and include only things you think that you will realistically sell. This may be an uphill battle with your business consultant.

Remember a sales representative's job is to sell to you. If the product company is inflexible and you have to buy the whole range, keep track of the slow sellers and reduce the price to ensure they sell more quickly. It is better to reduce the price to just above cost price, or even to cost price, than to see products get old and out of date and become unsellable. That would be a total waste of money.

Opening orders from reputable skincare companies often range in cost between £2000 and £5000. Some companies are very selective in who they allow to take on their products. Many will not supply to mobile or home-based beauty therapists. A typical launch package of a well-known product should contain the following:

- □ Two or three of each retail product

- □ One of each professional product

- □ Posters and other point-of-sale merchandising material

- □ Brochures, leaflets and other promotional material about the range

- □ Consultation and prescription cards

- □ Samples of the products

- □ Tester unit complete with testers

- □ Training manual and DVD

- □ Training for all staff

- □ Help and support for your launch event

- □ On-going services of a business support manager (your allocated sales rep).

Mail order or wholesale brand ranges

Wholesalers and mail order suppliers will have several low-cost professional ranges. They offer a useful alternative to the big-name brands for the mobile, home-based or student therapist. Two of the most popular brands are Salon System and Strictly Professional, which offer comprehensive and reasonably priced ranges.

THE PROS AND CONS OF BUYING MAIL ORDER OR WHOLESALE

Pros

☐ Low cost with no minimum order

☐ Cheaper than well known branded ranges

☐ Can be ordered or purchased from your wholesaler as and when needed

☐ You can buy just part of the range to suit the needs and requirements of your business

Cons

☐ Unknown brand to the public so little brand loyalty or recognition

☐ Limited marketing and promotional support

Wholesalers

When opening your own business you will find one of the most useful places to buy the everyday products and items for the salon are cash and carry beauty wholesalers. There are lots around the country; some are independent stockists and others are part of a chain such as Sally's. Wholesalers have the following advantages:

☐ They all stock a wide range of equipment and products.

☐ You are able to go in and buy what you need when you need it and take it away with you.

☐ They are competitively priced.

☐ There is no minimum order, which helps budgeting.

☐ They sell only to the trade.

☐ Some of them deliver weekly.

☐ An account can be opened allowing for 30 days' credit (subject to credit checks), which is useful for your cash flow.

There are also several companies that produce catalogues and you can buy online or over the phone. This is often the cheapest way of purchasing frequently-used items but you may have to buy in bulk. Consider if you have the space for storing these items before ordering. They may also have a minimum order for delivery, although this is usually quite reasonable. The following are a few you could try:

www.capitalhairandbeauty.co.uk

www.beautyexpress.co.uk

www.sallyexpress.com

The stock shop: 0208 361 8949

Producing your own branded products

This must be the dream of every beauty therapist. To see your own name or the name of your business on the side of a pot of skin cream. This dream is not as difficult to achieve as you may think. There are several companies that will discuss with you your ideas, source ingredients and packaging and will manufacture the product under your own label.

THE ADVANTAGES OF OWN-LABEL PRODUCTS

☐ They will add prestige to you and your business.

☐ They will enhance your professional identity and brand.

☐ They will enable you to gain a much higher profit margin from their sales.

☐ They will be unique and exclusive.

☐ You have full control of the ingredients and the manufacture of the products.

☐ You have creative control over the appearance and packaging of the range.

☐ Your range can adapt and grow according to your needs.

☐ There are good opportunities for future business growth from the sale and distribution of your products to other therapists.

Remember to ensure that you have adequate insurance for product liability. This will protect you in case of claims arising from the use of your products, such as an adverse reaction to an ingredient. The premiums for Product Liability Insurance may be high but are essential. Contact your professional association or a specialist insurance broker for advice and quotes.

To find manufacturers of 'own label' or 'private label' cosmetics and skincare lines, look on the internet or attend beauty trade shows either here or abroad. There are many companies who are active in this field. Make sure that you compare costs and service and what kind of contract they offer. Have clear ideas on the ingredients that you want to include and what results you want to achieve. Do your research on your clientèle and try to remain focused on what sector of the market you are hoping to appeal to. Finally, don't forget to keep an eye on your costs – the product must offer something that people want and must be able to compete in the market.

Buying your products

The basic products that you will be ordering on a regular basis for everyday use can be divided into four sections. Try to find the cheapest source (not the cheapest product) for each one. Time spent finding cheaper suppliers will pay dividends (literally!) in the long run when you do your end of year accounts.

GENERAL PRODUCTS

☐ Cotton wool

☐ Cotton buds

☐ Tissues

☐ Cleaning materials such as bleach and toilet rolls

☐ Tea, coffee, sugar

These items are best purchased from a general cash and carry such as Costco or Makro, where you will be able to buy in bulk.

BEAUTY PRODUCTS

☐ Couch roll

☐ Paper towels

☐ Gauze

☐ Spatulas

☐ Gloves (powdered are best for waxing as they will not stick)

The best prices for these items are found on medical wholesale websites especially if you have the room to store them if you order in bulk. Look at www.justgloves.co.uk and www.gompels.co.uk, but there are lots of others to check online.

WAX AND NAILS

☐ Wax: hot and strip

☐ Acetone

☐ Wax equipment cleaner

☐ Non-acetone nail varnish remover

☐ Nail files and polishers

☐ Waxing strips, paper and material

☐ Nail polishes

Non-branded items can be bought at a beauty wholesaler or online on a weekly, fortnightly or monthly basis as dictated by the needs of your business.

BRANDED AND MAIN RANGE PRODUCTS

If you use a branded range of products such as OPI, Toma or Essie for your nail treatments then these can also be bought from wholesalers or online, or you can order direct from the company. You will find that there is not much difference in price.

Order your main branded items such as your skincare range directly from the company, usually on a monthly basis. You will not only be ordering your treatment supplies, but also the retail products you have sold in the previous month. Make sure you order enough so that you always have a minimum of two of each product in stock. Generally speaking, there should be three kept in stock for popular items and six in stock for your best sellers.

Have an Order Book which is kept in a convenient place such as your store room or at the reception where everyone can write down what needs to be ordered as your supplies go down or you sell out of a line. Designate one person to place orders to avoid duplications.

Equipment and furniture

The choice of equipment and furniture in your salon depends largely on:

- ☐ The size of your salon.

- ☐ What treatments you will be offering.

- ☐ The theme of your salon.

- ☐ The amount of money available (your budget).

Make sure you examine, test and try, compare a few makes, and negotiate before you buy any of your equipment or furniture. The ideal place will be at a trade show or exhibition in the UK where you can get better discounts.

Treatment room essentials

Most of the expensive equipment will go into your treatment rooms. The very minimum equipment that you will need will consist of:

TREATMENT COUCH

Ideally this should be fully adjustable so that the head can be raised or the end lowered for the comfort of both the client and the therapist. The couch is probably the most important single item in the treatment room. Test several before purchasing one that is comfortable for the client to lie on and for you to use to avoid backache or strain. Make sure that your couch is adjustable for height. If your budget allows, an electric couch which is fully height adjustable by pressing a button is the ultimate to aim for.

STOOL

Any stool you choose must be fully adjustable for height and comfortable to sit on for long periods. The kneeling and saddle stools are recent arrivals which are excellent for maintaining good posture for the therapist, preventing back pain.

TROLLEYS

You may need several trolleys in your treatment room according to what treatments you are planning to offer. They should be made of materials which can be cleaned easily, such as aluminium or Formica. Trolleys need constant cleaning and should be able to withstand bleach and wax solvent. All trolleys should also be on wheels for ease of movement during treatment and cleaning of the room.

One should be a waxing trolley large enough to fit two wax pots or a double waxing unit (one for strip wax and one for hot); a container for your spatulas and scissors; small egg-cup sized container for your tweezers to be kept soaking in a barbicide solution; waxing strips (paper and material); talc; pre- and post-wax lotions or oils; powdered gloves and disposable G-strings. An illuminated magnifying lamp attached to the trolley will not only give you good light in which to wax but also magnification for finding missed hair.

SHELVES AND CUPBOARDS

Shelves are very useful for display and some storage, and a cupboard is good for putting things away to give an uncluttered look.

 Take accurate measurements of your rooms and all the equipment you intend to buy *before* ordering to make sure that everything will fit comfortably.

Waxing equipment

It is preferable to have two wax pots or a double pot in your treatment room, thereby giving both the therapist and the client a choice of which wax to use. This is particularly helpful when dealing with a different range of hair and hair growth, as each type of wax has its own pros and cons. The wax heaters should be thermostatically controlled to maintain the correct temperature throughout the day. They should be easily cleanable, have an outer casing that remains cool to the touch and be correctly wired and earthed.

An increasingly popular method of applying warm wax is with a roller which is stored in a heated container to maintain its correct temperature. The advantage of this method is that it is quick; however, rollers are more expensive to buy than wax sold in pots. The average price of wax heaters is between £40 and £100.

Electrolysis machines

There is strong customer demand for permanent hair removal so it is worthwhile investing in an electrolysis machine. Compare the different machines on the market and get recommendations from those who are using them.

Electrolysis machines can cost anything from £150 to £500, but the running costs are low. However, before you decide to buy one, make sure that you or at least one member of your staff is fully qualified to give the treatment. Although laser treatment has cut the demand for electrolysis, it is still a popular treatment and well worth the investment.

Laser and IPL machines

Lasers can successfully be used for permanent hair removal, pigmentation, acne, veins and for photo-rejuvenation. There are several types of laser currently available, including IPL, Ruby, Alexandrite, Diode and Nd Yag.

IPL (Intense Pulse Light) is not strictly a laser but it uses the same principles and is similar in use and effect. It successfully reduces hair growth by emitting pulses of light which destroy the pigment in the hair follicle. These machines have the following features:

☐ They are considered the safest and most effective method of hair removal and hair reduction on the market, with very few side effects.

☐ They can be used to treat most skin colours from very pale to dark (Fitzwilliam scale 1 to 5).

☐ They are less effective on darker skin types or on pale hair.

☐ The same machine can be used for different treatments with just the addition of an extra hand piece, although it is most effective for hair reduction and pigmentation.

☐ IPL machines are very easy to use.

☐ Using larger head sizes which cover a wider treatment area makes treatment quicker than by other methods.

Ruby is the oldest laser method used for hair removal and offers the following features:

☐ It has a long track record for the successful removal of hair but its technology has been overtaken by newer machines.

☐ It is relatively less painful than other types of laser.

☐ Its small head size makes it slow to cover large areas.

☐ Ruby lasers cannot be used on darker complexions or fair hair.

☐ There is some risk of burns, scars and hypo (lightening) and hyper (darkening) pigmentation problems.

Alexandrite is probably one of the most widely available laser machines. Its features include:

☐ Fast treatment times so excellent for large areas such as legs.

☐ Good reduction rate for finer hairs which can be difficult to treat with other methods.

☐ Can be used to treat only fair to olive skin and is unsuitable for darker skin tones.

Diode has a longer wavelength and is therefore able to treat darker skins. It includes the following features:

☐ It has been used long term and has been proved to give safe and effective hair reduction for all six skin tones.

☐ It has some risk of pigmentation, burns, urticaria or redness post-treatment but these problems are usually transient.

☐ It can cover large areas quickly.

Nd Yag is another long-pulse laser which can safely treat darker complexions. Its features include:

☐ It is fairly new to the market, so long-term results and safety have not been fully assessed.

☐ It is quick to use and can cover larger areas.

☐ Good results can be seen on dark hair and skin tones but less effective on fine or fair hair.

☐ It is reputedly more painful than other methods.

Should I invest in laser?

The use of laser and IPL machines has become widespread in beauty salons. Many salon owners are talked into spending tens of thousands of pounds without doing proper research. If you have the space and resources, laser is an excellent business investment, but it would be wise to consider the following first:

☐ Is there a demand for laser treatment from your clients? Are your waxing clients asking you about this new technology? Do research in your area and find out if people are interested before you decide to buy a machine.

☐ Give serious consideration to the costs involved. Lasers are expensive to buy and run. There are increased training and insurance costs, the initial costs of registration with the Care Quality Commission (formally the Healthcare Commission; the CQC is an independent regulator of healthcare standards to ensure the safe use of and good practice for laser treatments), and then the yearly membership fee, as well as the continuous cost of appointing a Laser Protection Adviser (LPA) and Expert Medical Practitioner (EMP).

☐ Investigate the additional cost of converting a room to meet the special safety requirements of the local council and the Care Quality Commission.

☐ There are also increased legal requirements associated with operating a laser in a safe environment and registering with the Care Quality Commission, and this will result in you spending a lot more time on paperwork.

☐ There is no doubt that lasers are popular with the public, are giving excellent results and the addition of a laser to your salon could result in increased income and turnover for your business.

How to choose a laser machine

Buying a laser or IPL machine is a major investment and will require a great deal of research and investigation. The following list will help you make this very important decision:

☐ Choose the type of laser to suit your clientèle and business. Consider if you need a machine that can be used on darker skin tones or is effective on finer or fairer hair.

☐ Do your research. The market is saturated with companies offering different machines from all over the world. A great place to start is the beauty trade exhibitions, where most companies will be promoting their machines. Read their brochures, compare machines and ask for a demonstration.

☐ Talk to the company's advisers and ask the following questions:

– What are the technical specifications of the laser/IPL machine?

– How long has the machine been on the market?

– How successful is it for permanent reduction in hair growth? What evidence is there to support their claim?

– How safe is the machine, and what evidence do they offer?

– What levels of support do they offer if the machine breaks down? Do they offer a replacement machine within 24 hours?

– What is their breakdown and maintenance cover programme and what is the cost?

– What is the average life of each lamp and what is the replacement cost?

– Do they offer training and if so at what cost? Can new staff be trained as and when needed without charge?

– Does the company provide Care Quality Commission registration support? Is there a charge for this?

– Will the company provide a Laser Protection Adviser and Expert Medical Practitioner? Is this service free?

– Can they provide marketing and promotional materials together with client record cards, detailed client information leaflets and legal indemnity waver forms?

– How long is the warranty and what does it cover?

– What is the cost of the machine?

The above questions are extremely important in your decision-making process.

 One very useful way of making comparisons is to make a chart with all the above questions across the top and all the companies' names on the left. Then fill the squares in the chart. This way, at a glance you can make a quick comparison. A sample is shown in Figure 7.1

☐ Once you have narrowed down your choice to three or four, find out who uses these machines and if possible visit and talk to them. Otherwise make a telephone call and discuss it over the phone with the owners. Most people will be more than happy to tell you of their experience.

☐ Find out and compare the increased costs for insurance.

☐ Contact the CQC at www.cqc.org.uk and ask them for their information pack. Also contact your local council and see what their requirements are.

☐ There are several companies that provide a complete laser support service for an annual fee and they are very useful when you are first registering with the Care Quality Commission and the subsequent requirements for a LPA and EMP. One of the biggest companies in this field is www.lasermet.com which provides ongoing risk assessments and all the policies and procedures required for an annual fee of approximately £1,250. However, some laser/IPL manufacturers will provide this service free of charge for the first year, if you buy their machine.

☐ When you have narrowed your laser/IPL machines down to the final three models you can start negotiating the price. Many companies offer instalments, hire purchase, leasing or other incentives to buy.

 Before finalising the purchase of your laser/IPL machine, add up the initial costs of the machine as well as the annual running costs. Make sure that you can make money from adding this machine to your salon by pricing the treatments correctly while remaining competitive with other salons in your area.

Company	Cost	Warranty	Lamp cost	Lamp life	Service cost	Years on the market	No. of staff training	Training on/off site	Care quality Comm. support yes/no cost	L.P.A. yes/no cost
A										
B										
C										
D										
E										
F										
G										

Notes:

Figure 7.1 Company comparison chart

ESTIMATED COSTS

Machine	£5,000–£50,000
Registration Fee with CQC	£1,500 (annual)
Laser support services (LPA Laser Protection Adviser)	£1,250 (annual)
Adapting room	£1,500
Extra insurance	£200 (annual)
Cost of lamp replacement	£500–£750 after every 20,000 flashes

Plus repair charges after the expiry of the warranty.

Facial equipment

There are several types of machine offering specialised treatments for the skin. These machines target skin problems. However, not all the machines are worth the investment. One way of saving money and space is to buy a combined unit which is also portable. This is useful if you have to give treatment outside the salon.

HIGH-FREQUENCY MACHINES

These machines use a high-frequency current (an oscillating current) which is applied either directly or indirectly for its therapeutic effects on the skin. Although considered to be a very effective and useful item of equipment for the skincare professional, it has nevertheless gone out of fashion in recent times. It offers very effective treatment for spots, oily skin and acne and is invaluable for its stimulating and germicidal properties on all skin types. The average cost is £100 to £300.

 **High-frequency machines provide a low-cost but very effective treatment for a variety of skin types.**

GALVANIC MACHINES (DESINCRUSTATION AND IONTIPHORESIS)

Galvanic machines use a galvanic current to deep-cleanse the skin – desincrustation – and to introduce active substances chosen for their specific properties into the skin – iontiphoresis. It is a very successful way of treating the skin and can give amazing results in skilled hands. The average cost of a machine is £300 to £800.

 Using a galvanic machine is a specialised skill and should be considered only as an essential item for skincare specialists.

STEAMER

An ozone steamer is the most popular form of facial electrical equipment used in beauty therapy. The steam produced cleanses and softens the skin prior to extraction, while the ozone is anti-bacterial. The machine comes in a variety of sizes, ranging from small hand-held devices, to larger tabletop models, to stand-alone fully adjustable models. Make sure you consider the size of the treatment room when you are choosing a steamer as some models can take up a large amount of space. The cost varies between £50 and £500.

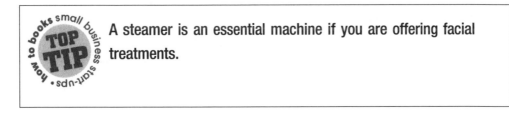 A steamer is an essential machine if you are offering facial treatments.

HOT TOWEL CABINET

The addition of hot towels to remove products during facial and body treatments adds a touch of luxury and pampering compared with the sponges and tepid water of the past. The feeling of being enveloped in warm, fresh towels infused with lavender essential oils adds that extra-special something to your facials. The use of warm towels at the end of a massage or to remove bodycare products instantly relaxes the client and finishes off the treatment perfectly.

There are several models of towel heater on the market, from those holding 20 or more towels to more compact models for smaller therapy rooms. The average cost of a cabinet is between £100 and £200.

 A hot towel cabinet is a strongly recommended addition to your salon from day one.

Micro-dermabrasion

Micro-dermabrasion machines blast the skin's surface with crystals which are then sucked away leaving the skin exfoliated. This treatment is very popular and often asked for by clients. The machine, if used correctly, can offer beneficial results for acne, sun damage, scarring and pigmentation.

These machines can be very expensive but can give an excellent return on your investment in the long run.

There are several well-known brands such as Crystal Clear available to the skincare therapist. Most of the bigger companies have invested in advertising and websites aimed at bringing clients to your business, so it could be worth the increased costs associated with purchasing their machines.

However, there are many less well-known makes of machine available at lower prices if you feel that cost is an important consideration.

If you decide to buy a machine for this treatment, make sure of the following:

- □ Ask for a demonstration of the machine and get a feel for it.

- □ Consider training costs that will be necessary for your employees.

- □ Find out the costs of the crystals and other items used in the treatments.

- □ Find out how reliable the machine is and how easy it is to maintain.

Micro-dermabrasion machines can cost anything from £1,500 to £8,000, plus the cost of the crystals.

> **TOP TIP** Micro-dermabrasion is quite a popular treatment. It is not an essential machine but is a potentially lucrative addition to your salon if you can afford it.

Micro-current

Micro-current machines are relatively new. The treatment was first used by doctors and physiotherapists for the treatment of facial muscle weakness and Bell's palsy. However, it has been used cosmetically since the 1980s to tighten and tone facial muscles, stimulate collagen and drain lymphatic fluid, rejuvenating the face. Clients

177

are required to have a course of treatments and with a skilled therapist the results can be impressive.

There are several well-known brands of micro-current machine which are frequently mentioned in the beauty magazines. Clients frequently ask for these machines by name so consider this when weighing up whether to buy a well-known make or a cheaper unknown brand.

 The initial costs can be very high – as much as £2,000 to £10,000 – but it is a popular treatment with customers who will return on a regular basis.

Oxygen treatment machines

Oxygen therapy treatments are frequently combined with micro-dermabrasion, and involve blasting the skin with pressurised air applied through a tube, allowing the penetration of serums containing vitamins and hyaluronic acid to plump out fine lines and wrinkles. This stimulates cell regeneration, giving a glowing, youthful appearance to the skin.

This treatment has had a lot of exposure in the press in the last few years, creating much demand.

The machine can be expensive to purchase. If you decide to buy one, make sure that you check the running costs as well as the warranty and breakdown cover.

The setting-up costs of this kind of machine can be anything from £2,000 to £10,000, but the results are normally impressive.

 As it is not yet clear where this technology will be in, say, five years' time. Think carefully before investing in something which could possibly turn out to be a short-term fad.

Micro-pigmentation

Micro-pigmentation is also known as semi-permanent make-up or cosmetic tattooing. A fine needle tattoos a line around the lips, eyes or eyebrows, thus enhancing these features. The technique can also be used to restore the areola on the nipple and to cover scars. The pigments fade over time but usually last up to three years.

The equipment and training for this treatment is very costly, but it is an investment with high returns. A qualified technician in this field can earn as much as £300 per hour of work.

The average cost of training and equipment can vary enormously and be as much as £5,000 to £10,000.

Equipment for body treatments

Body treatments are very popular and are an essential addition to your beauty salon. Apart from the various massage techniques, it is worthwhile investing to further your skills and training to include specialist machines.

IONITHERMIE

Ionithermie is a firming, toning body treatment that reduces the appearance of cellulite. The treatment machine uses two electrical currents – galvanic and faradic – to stimulate muscle contractions and to introduce biologically-active ingredients while the client is being covered with thermal algae clay. Each treatment is the equivalent of 800 sit-ups and the recommended course is one treatment a week for five weeks. The results are consistently good, with most clients returning throughout the year. Treatment with an ionithermie machine offers the following features:

☐ It is most suitable for clients within a stone of their ideal weight, for post-weight-loss toning or for spot reduction.

☐ It involves a one-week training programme at the company's headquarters in Windsor.

☐ The machine is compact, portable and suitable for a small treatment room.

☐ The treatment itself can be messy. However, shower facilities are not required in the salon.

The approximate cost of an ionithermie machine is about £3,000.

ENDERMOLOGIE

Endermologie is a deep tissue massage machine that helps reduce the appearance of cellulite. The machine uses a combination of deep massage and vacuum suction to increase lymph drainage and break down fatty deposits. Endermologie was pioneered in France in the 1990s and has since been approved by the American Food and Drug Agency (FDA).

This is a major investment, with costs in excess of £25,000. However, it gives good results in clients more than a stone overweight or with solid visible cellulite.

You should note that endermologie has been described as painful or uncomfortable and may result in temporary bruising to the area of treatment.

 An endermologie machine is very expensive to buy and set up. Endermologie should be considered only by premium salons that can afford and get a return on their investment.

G5

G5 is a massage machine with five attachments that gyrate and vibrate, providing a variety of massage techniques for deep tissue work, cellulite reduction or muscle relaxation. It helps to break down fat, increase circulation and smooth and tone the skin. If you are considering the use of this machine in your salon, it is worth noting that:

☐ The therapist needs to have an NVQ 3 to use a G5 massager. Most therapists are trained in its use as part of their beauty therapy training so there are no additional training costs involved with purchasing the machine.

☐ Correctly used, the machine gives excellent results and provides a relaxing and enjoyable treatment.

☐ The G5 has been used in beauty therapy for many years and although it has gone out of fashion in recent times, it still offers a great additional service for a low financial outlay.

The average cost of a machine is about £600.

 G5 is a good-value treatment for a salon wishing to offer basic cellulite or massage treatments.

FARADIC

There are several machines which use a faradic current to stimulate the muscles to contract. Modern machines often use a combination of electrical currents, making the treatment more comfortable for the client. Between each surge of current there is a rest, during which no current flows, allowing the muscle to relax. Each session commonly has about 800 contractions – far more than can be achieved in the gym in the same time – making this treatment ideal for people unable to do conventional exercise or for intensive spot reduction and toning.

The placing of the pads can be complex, requiring knowledge of the muscle groups and motor points. Therapists who have obtained NVQ 3 or equivalent will have been taught this as part of their training, so training costs on the machine can be kept to a minimum.

There are several well-known brands of machine such as Slendertone, Ultratone and Silhouette on the market, as well as Carlton and Skinmate. Compare prices for start-up packages to see what is included.

There is a variety of these machines costing between £1,000 and £5,000.

Sunbeds

Sunbeds have had a bad press in recent times but this does not seem to have dimmed their popularity. Clients still want to get a tan for that special occasion, holiday or just to feel good, despite the known health risks.

If you are seriously considering including this treatment in your salon, be aware of the following facts:

☐ 7% of the UK population regularly uses sunbeds – that is over 3 million people.

☐ Many in the health and beauty industry would see the use of a sunbed in a salon or clinic as compromising the high standards of the industry.

☐ If you decide to install a machine, join the Sunbed Association. Look at its informative website at www.sunbedassociation.org.uk It has a code of practice that all members must adhere to and gives support and advice to its members.

☐ Sunbeds can be rented from around £100 a week and can generate a revenue of approximately £30 per hour, so they can produce a profit very quickly. A lot of salons rent machines.

If you have unused space in your salon, adding a sunbed could generate big profits quickly with minimal outlay or staffing costs.

Spray tanning machines

Self-tanning lotions have greatly improved from the old-fashioned messy creams that gave people an orange glow and made them smell for days. The new generation of fake tans smell better, are quick and easy to apply and give a great natural colour. These machines have the following features:

☐ The self-tanner can be applied quickly in 10 minutes with an airbrush either by a therapist or in an automated machine.

☐ This treatment is very popular with clients who will frequently ask for brand leaders such as St Tropez or Fake Bake, so consider this brand awareness when comparing suppliers. Other brands often offer cheaper but just as good self-tanning products so try before you buy.

☐ The automated machines are large but are easy to maintain and run, requiring minimal staff involvement. They are also expensive to buy and are often leased. Consider what your likely income from the machine will be before committing, as the demand for fake tans ebbs and flows with the time of year.

☐ The smaller salon can use a shower or small treatment room for the therapist-operated spray tanning machines. However, the room will require constant cleaning as the tan gets everywhere! Pop-up tents are useful for minimising this overspray and good ventilation is essential.

☐ Training in the use of the machine is very quick and can easily be achieved in a morning, followed by some practice.

The average cost of the airbrush machines is around £100. The automated ones will cost as much as £2,000.

Spray tanning is a highly recommended treatment for your salon. You will get an excellent return on your investment with this quick, easy and very popular treatment.

Nail equipment

The basic equipment required for carrying out nail services is:

☐ A manicure table,

☐ A pedicure chair,

☐ A stool,

☐ A nail trolley.

If you want to create a luxurious impression, there is a variety of very impressive equipment available. Consider carefully how to spend your budget as it is easy to get carried away with top-of-the-range furniture.

When buying your furniture for nail treatments you should consider the following:

☐ How much use will the item have? If you do only ten pedicures a week, can you justify spending £1,200 on a pedicure chair? If you do ten a day, then the cost is justified.

☐ Does it reflect the ethos of your salon? A 'Las Vegas'-style flashy chair would look out of place in a natural product salon.

☐ Do you have adequate room? Always take your room measurements to exhibitions, and don't forget the ceiling height.

☐ Can you save money here to use elsewhere?

MANICURE TABLE

Look for a manicure table that is stable and solid, made from an easily cleanable surface. Make sure the surface is not easy to damage if scratched or in contact with solvents, as some plastics can stain when splashed with acetone. A lamp that can be swung overhead is great for illuminating the nails during treatment. A filter is useful if you are planning to do acrylic nails as the dust can be removed. The average cost is £70 to £400.

PEDICURE CHAIR

These can be basic such as a comfortable elevated chair with a simple platform for the pedicure bowl and an adjustable footrest allowing a strain-free working position for the therapist.

Some of the deluxe chairs on the market are amazing and are often imported from the Far East or America. They can give your business the 'wow factor' but bear in mind the following points:

☐ Many come with inbuilt plumbing for the foot spa so make sure that there is suitable plumbing near the chair.

☐ The drains need constant cleaning and can get easily blocked with toenails.

☐ Cleaning must be thorough and consistent, as germs and bacteria can get blocked in the jets, causing infections and bad smells.

☐ Look into the guarantee and service aspects of your purchase.

☐ Consider how much use you will get from such an expensive model before you commit yourself to buying one.

The average cost is £200 to £2,000.

NAIL TROLLEY AND STOOL

The trolley containing all your nail products will need to be on wheels so that it can easily be moved around. Make sure that it's easy to keep clean with plenty of shelves or drawers for storage of the nail varnishes and other requisites. Another solution is to put all the polishes in a display in the reception area for the client to choose from. This presents an ideal opportunity for retailing the matching colour to the client after their manicure or pedicure. The average cost is £50 to £200.

Mobile therapy equipment

The needs and requirements of the mobile therapist are different from those of the salon. Occasionally you may get special requests for a home visit, and if possible you should be able to offer some of your treatments. The equipment needed should be:

☐ Portable

☐ Compact

☐ Light to carry

☐ Insured.

After the essential purchases you will need a reliable mode of transport, usually a car with a secure boot to carry the equipment out of sight. But another great way to get to your clients would be on a motorbike or scooter. They are quick, economical to run and easy to park, and perfect if you don't need to carry much equipment for treatments such as nails and massage.

 Remember to keep all your receipts for petrol, repairs and maintenance, tax and insurance of your vehicle to claim as expenses when completing your tax return.

PORTABLE EQUIPMENT

The following is a list of essential equipment for mobile therapists and therapists making visits outside the salon:

☐ Lightweight yet sturdy massage table. The best are super-light aluminium but make sure the table is solid even with a large client lying on it. The slightly heavier hardwood table with locking leg struts may be more sturdy – important to consider if you are planning to do massage.

☐ Portable trolley.

☐ Portable manicure table.

☐ Small travel suitcases are a great way to transport facial skincare products and nail equipment. There are several specially made for the mobile therapist or check your local bag and luggage store.

☐ Hand-held portable steamer.

Most facial equipment, such as high-frequency, galvanic, micro-dermabrasion or micro-current, come in small portable units. Try to get a combined unit which will save you having to carry lots of pieces of equipment.

Second-hand equipment

Purchasing second-hand beauty furniture and equipment is a useful option if your finances are very limited when you are just starting your business. Although the choice may be limited to what is available at the time, leaving you with little scope to choose colours or design, the opportunity is there to pick up a great piece of equipment at a fraction of the original cost. This is mainly applicable to larger and more expensive items. However, there are some very important points to consider:

☐ Find out the age and condition of the item you intend to buy.

☐ Check to see if all the attachments are still available.

☐ See if the item is still covered by the manufacturer's warranty, and if it is, can it be transferred to a new owner?

☐ Obtain a full service history if possible.

☐ Will you be able to get training arranged on the machine? If the machine is complicated to operate, then this should preferably be done by the manufacturer.

☐ Can you get insurance cover for using it?

☐ Ask why the item is being sold. The answer often reveals a lot. Read between the lines of their answer; if they say that the business is closing down, could this be due to the fact that the equipment is not being very effective and not achieving results? (This is particularly important for expensive items such as laser machines.)

☐ Notice if there are a lot of the same machines for sale on the second-hand market. This could be due to problems with the machine. This indicates either a poor performance machine, a problem with breakdowns or high running costs.

☐ Put the equipment to the test and see if it does what it is supposed to do.

☐ Make sure that you can easily contact the seller if you encounter problems with the machine.

☐ An ex-demo item offered for sale by the supplier is often a good investment but make sure you check for damage as the item will usually be offered for sale as seen.

☐ Finally, make sure to take all the usual precautions when purchasing from an unknown private seller or online.

When buying second-hand equipment make sure you negotiate hard – you can save a lot of money this way.

For good information and bargains, visit www.startinbusiness.co.uk, www.salonstuff.co.uk and www.ebay.co.uk

Renting equipment

There are several companies that rent beauty equipment and furniture, right down to the tables and stools. This is perfect if you are trying to keep your start-up costs low. However, in the long term it is an expensive way to acquire items. The advantages are that you can try out items before buying them, and you may be able to upgrade machines, such as IPL, as new models come onto the market.

Leasing or hire purchase

Most manufacturers of expensive machines and equipment offer leasing or hire-purchase arrangements either directly or through a finance house. Once again this is an option if you need the item in question but cannot afford to buy it outright.

Although there is a small tax advantage in claiming your VAT back, you should note that the amount of interest paid over the term of the lease or the hire purchase will be substantially more than what you save.

This is not a recommended option as the leasing and hire-purchase companies normally charge very high interest rates for the money they lend you to make your purchase. If you have to buy and have to raise money for the purchase, then a bank loan will be a much better way of financing your purchase.

Buying furniture

Generally speaking, your salon will not need a lot of furniture. The main items are:

- ☐ A desk or counter for the reception.

- ☐ Depending on the style and design of your salon, a chair for the receptionist.

- ☐ A few comfortable chairs for the waiting room.

- ☐ One or two small tables for the waiting room.

☐ Two or three chairs for the staff room.

☐ One chair for every treatment room.

You should also of course have a good-quality commercial washing machine and a dryer, costing from £1,000 to £1,500.

 Your furniture must blend in with the design, look and colour scheme of your salon.

8
BUSINESS MANAGEMENT

IN THIS CHAPTER

- [ ] What are your business objectives?

- [ ] Putting together your business plan

- [ ] Keeping the cash flowing

- [ ] Knowing how to manage

- [ ] Staying in control

- [ ] The advantages of being computerised

- [ ] Getting through the tough times

In Chapter 3 we discussed the day-to-day running of the salon and what is needed for its smooth operation. However, the management of your beauty business involves much more than just the salon itself and requires effective management skills.

Most beauty therapists never receive direct education or training in management, which, when they start their own business, invariably creates problems that they find difficult to handle and resolve. In this chapter we will cover the essential skills needed to ensure the smooth running of the business and will illustrate what management skills are needed for the ultimate success of your beauty business.

Having objectives and a plan

Understanding the jargon used in business is often helpful. Words such as 'plan', 'policy', 'objective', 'mission', 'vision', etc. are commonly used and can be quite confusing if not fully understood. The following simple explanations clarify the meanings of some common terms:

Policy: The guidelines which describe the rules and regulations.

Mission: The purpose of a business.

Vision: The intended future direction of the business; where it is intended to go.

Objective: What the business is aiming to achieve or gain.

Strategy: The co-ordinated plan of action of a business.

When you are starting a business, or in fact any project, you need a plan of what you are going to do and you must set out what your objectives are. Without these two, it is like driving a car blindfolded, to an unknown destination. You will certainly not get very far before disaster strikes.

It is estimated that one in three new businesses fails in its first year, mainly due to lack of proper planning.

Before you do anything, you must decide why you want to have your own salon and what you hope to achieve from having and running it. Then you must create a plan of how you are going to achieve this.

EXAMPLE

Let's say you need a rain coat. To get one, you must go shopping. You decide to go to Bluewater shopping centre and buy a rain coat. We can then say:

Your plan is *to go to Bluewater shopping centre*.

Your objective is *to buy a rain coat*.

What are your business objectives?

Your business objectives will be unique to your business and should be divided into three parts; short term, medium term and long term. Each one will form a blueprint or framework for your business.

For your business to succeed, your objectives must be factual, realistic, achievable, assessable and measurable.

In the above example, if you lived 10 miles away from Bluewater shopping centre and you had only half an hour to do the shopping, we can say that your objective is not achievable. Your plan will not work as it is not realistic in the short time available to you.

Even if you clearly know what your objectives are and how you are going to achieve them, make sure they are all *written down* and expressed in a clear and concise manner. You will need to refer to these objectives regularly to see if you are on course and if your objectives are being achieved.

In Chapter 1 we talked about your business plan and its important role in starting your beauty business. The significance of producing and using your plan should not be underestimated. For this reason we now look further into business plans.

Writing your business plan

Once you are clear about your objectives and have gathered information which relates to your proposed ideas, you should begin writing your business plan. The main topics to be included were discussed in Chapter 1. The following is a list of other subjects which must be referred to and included in your business plan:

☐ The business name, address, telephone number, e-mail address, fax number (if you have one) and website address.

☐ Details and experience of people involved in the business.

☐ What your market is going to cover.

☐ The nature of your business and what your business is going to do.

☐ The outline of your marketing and advertising ideas and strategy.

☐ A survey of the competition in your area.

☐ A projection of your capital expenditure (set-up cost) for starting the business.

☐ A monthly forecast of your income and all your expected outgoings and expenses for the first three years (cash-flow forecast).

☐ Your turnover and profit/loss forecast for the first three years.

☐ Details of how much money you are putting into the business, and how much you need to raise, if any.

☐ How and over what period you intend to repay your loan, if you have one.

There are many websites which give you examples of how to write a proper business plan — make use of them. The following short, basic example of a hypothetical business plan also shows a financial forecast.

Proposed Business Plan for Beauty 4 You

Name of business: Beauty 4 You

Nature of business: Beauty Salon

Objective: To provide a range of beauty treatments and related products, including waxing, sunless tanning, manicure and pedicure, and facials at mid-range prices.

Business address: 22 High Street, Cotton Hill, Surrey B4 2BS

Tel. 01003 223399 *Mob.* 0970867547 *Fax.* 01003 456789

E-mail: beauty4you@something.co.uk

Website: www.beauty4you.co.uk

Type of business: Partnership

Partners: Miss Sandra Someone and Mrs Debbie Somebody

Number of staff: Four, including both partners

Staff qualifications and experience: Both partners are senior therapists with six years' experience, one with two years' managerial experience in a small beauty salon. The others will be chosen with a minimum of two years' experience and NVQ Level 3 qualification.

Locality: In the High Street, busy with shoppers, good residential in the surrounding areas, two bus routes, railway station 10 minutes' walk, excellent parking facilities with two large public car parks. Local hospital 20 minutes' walk. Many shops and offices nearby.

Opening: Estimated 1 July 201X.

The premises: Ground-floor shop, three rooms, toilet and store. Ten-year lease, £12,000/year rent, £4,200/year rates.

Opening hours: Monday–Saturday 9a.m. to 6.00p.m.

The market: Primarily 18–60 range of women and men.

Catchment area: Nearby office workers, which includes one very large firm of accountants and several smaller firms, the local hospital staff, and the local residents.

Competition: One hair and beauty salon, mainly hair, very limited beauty treatments; no retail of beauty products.

Initial marketing and advertising: Two opening adverts in the local paper; one very large poster in the window; 5,000 colour leaflets with 10% opening offer; one-day opening event with free consultations, free samples, soft drinks and nibbles.

Capital available: £15,000 from each partner. Total: £30,000

START-UP COSTS:

Premises (cost of lease, professional fees and deposit)	£15,000
Interior and exterior refurbishment and decoration, including security	£20,000
Salon furniture and decoration	£8,000
Treatment equipment, tools, uniforms, towels, etc.	£10,000
Stock	£4,000
Insurance, membership, licensing fees, etc.	£1,500
Miscellaneous (stationery, flower pots, CDs, etc.)	£1,000
Total:	£59,500

RUNNING COSTS (first year)

Rent and rates:	£16,200
Electricity, gas, water, telephone and internet, and waste collection	£3,200
Wages, including National Insurance contributions	£70,000
Transport, petrol, parking, car expenses	£4,000
Professional fees, licence fees and membership	£2,000
Repairs and renewals	£2,000
Bank loan repayment, bank charges and interest	£12,000
Training, seminars and courses	£1,000
Marketing, advertising and printing	£2,000
Miscellaneous (including float, petty cash, and other unexpected costs)	£5,000
Total:	£117,400

▶

The estimated running costs for the first six months will be half
of this (£117,400 ÷ 2)   £58,700

Grand total fund needed to start and run business for six months
(£59,500 + £58,700)   £118,200

Estimated weekly takings per week (assuming three therapists
working five days per week, each taking £175 per day; the fourth
will share the receptionist job).   £2,625

This gives total takings from treatments in the first six months
(allowing for bank holidays and Christmas and Easter
closures)   £65,625

Product sales (add)   + £4,000

Grand total takings in the first six months   £69,625

Less VAT payable (using standard rate of 17.5%, £10,370)   £59,255

Money available from partners   £30,000

Estimated total available during the first six months (sum of the
above two)   £89,255

Balance needed to borrow (£118,200 − £89,255)   £28,945

Rounding this up, a loan of £30,000 will be needed for this business
proposition, spread over three and a half years.

A simple cash flow for the first three years is shown below:

	Year 1	Year 2	Year 3
Rent and rates	£16,200	£16,400	£16,600
Utilities, telephone and waste	£3,200	£3,500	£3,800
Wages	£70,000	£77,000	£80,000
Transport and car	£4,000	£4,400	£4,600
Professional and membership fees	£2,000	£2,200	£2,500
Bank loan repayment	£12,000	£13,000	£14,000
Training and courses	£1,000	£1,200	£1,500
Advertising, marketing and printing	£2,000	£2,500	£3,000
Misc.	£5,000	£10,000	£10,000
(a) TOTAL OUTGOINGS	£115,400	£130,200	£136,000
(b) Estimated gross takings	£131,250	£170,000	£195,000
(c) Net of VAT takings	£111,702	£144,681	£165,958
(d) (c − a) = Gross Profit/(Loss)	(£3,700)	£14,181	£29,958

The above example is only a simple illustration of how your business plan and cash
flow can be constructed.

Make sure your plan is an honest and accurate account of your proposed business. If it is otherwise, it will inevitably be discovered by experienced investors and bankers.

Cash flow

Your business will survive and thrive only if money keeps coming in and in large enough amounts. If you don't have a good cash flow, problems will soon arise, as you will not be able to pay for your goods, services and everyone's wages. A cash-flow diagram clearly shows you how things are currently, and are likely to be in the months ahead. From such a diagram, a simple prediction can be made and if necessary corrective action can be taken before things get out of control.

You can easily construct cash-flow diagrams for the first six or twelve months as shown below. If your predictions are reasonably accurate, you can see the position of your bank balance in the months ahead ((f) Balance left):

	July	Aug.	Sept.	Oct.	Nov.	Dec.	Jan.	Feb.	Mar.	Apr.	May	June
(a) Cash in bank												
(b) Treatment sales												
(c) Product sales												
(d) Total sum available (a+b+c)												
(e) Total running costs												
(f) Balance left (d−e)												

Once you are clear about your overall objectives and have written a plan for your business, you need to develop objectives and plans for your salon. These may sound complex, but they are not. Here are some typical objectives which may be relevant to a beauty salon business:

☐ To create a relaxing atmosphere

☐ To give every client a warm welcome

☐ To have friendly and helpful staff

☐ To offer specialist treatments

☐ To make every client feel they are special and satisfied when they leave

☐ To open outside office hours and weekends

☐ To aim at the middle end of the market (or upper or lower)

☐ To achieve a gross return of 20% on the investment (financial objective)

☐ To achieve a profit of £xxxxx (this figure will depend on the size and potential of your salon) within three years (financial objective).

 It is always nice to have something special, different or unique about your salon so that your clientèle will talk about it. This creates customer loyalty and often leads to recommendations to friends and family.

How to manage

Very often untrained people who run their own businesses believe management is about controlling their staff. The role of a manager is very involved and includes:

☐ Understanding the objective of the business.

☐ Being aware of changes in the industry.

☐ Being able to motivate, delegate to and lead staff under their management.

☐ Being able to control the direction in which the business is going.

☐ Being able to take decisive and corrective action when needed.

There are many definitions of management. In general it can be said that management operates through the collective action of the following functions:

☐ **Planning:** Deciding what needs to be done and what has to happen.

☐ **Organising:** Making arrangements for the efficient use of people, facilities and resources in order to carry out various tasks and achieve the best possible results.

☐ **Motivating:** Stimulating desire and interest, ensuring that your staff are happy and willing to do their jobs to the best of their ability.

☐ **Leading:** Finding out what has to be done and getting your staff to do it efficiently.

☐ **Controlling:** Monitoring the progress of a job or a project, and taking action to change or modify what is necessary to achieve the goal or objective against the plan, if and when necessary.

Effective management requires a series of skills. Some of these skills are naturally inherited, some are gained from experience in business, and others can be learned.

Being able to lead, the ability to be decisive, enjoying decision-making, being able to delegate, being a good listener, and being able to take control without being a control freak are some of the skills needed for good management of not only the salon but also the business as a whole.

 Do you feel that you can easily associate these skills with your own character? If not, you may well be advised to consider having a business partner who will manage the business while you run the salon, especially if you are going to continue in your role as a therapist.

 Good management also requires information. The more you know about your business, your staff, your clients and your competition, the better you can manage and control your business. Make sure you are always well informed.

When running a business, you will need to manage and control many things. Effective management of your beauty salon and your business as a whole will need good planning, organising, monitoring and controlling, all of which were discussed above.

The most important thing that needs to be planned, organised, monitored and controlled is your time. It is common to hear people who run their own business saying, 'I just don't have the time'.

For this reason, time management is a key element of running your business.

TIME MANAGEMENT

The majority of beauty salons are operated and managed by beauty therapists who continue to do treatments. Running a beauty business involves managing many things: the salon, the staff, the appointments, the stock, repairs, wages, the accounts, bills and much more, *and* still remaining positive, calm and happy. No wonder salon owners often complain of having no time.

Having inadequate time management and delegation skills will result in a lack of organisation which in turn creates chaos, affecting staff and clients. It produces immense stress, which in turn is reflected in one's health and personal life. This is why time management is probably the most important thing in running any business. Time management improves efficiency.

If you don't manage your time properly, you will have great difficulty managing anyone or anything else.

To manage your time effectively, there are several basic rules to follow:

☐ Prepare a list of everything which has to be done. Some are daily, others weekly and monthly.

☐ Produce a time-chart, or timetable and cross out jobs as they are done.

☐ Put jobs in order of urgency and deal with them in that order.

☐ Add new things which crop up in the right order of priority in the chart.

☐ Review your time-chart regularly, as sometimes priority and urgency change.

☐ Include in your time-chart, time for *yourself* to relax and do things that you enjoy.

☐ Make sure you stick to this routine no matter what happens.

Your time-chart should include time for paying bills, answering letters and e-mails, staff training, ordering stock and visits to wholesalers, stock control, renewing contracts, cleaning, repairs and renewals, staff meetings, daily accounts and banking.

STRESS MANAGEMENT

In order to operate good time management in your business, your life must be stress-free – something which is almost impossible. And to operate a stress-free business you need to manage the stresses of everyday life.

To avoid job-related stress:

☐ Make sure you employ well-trained, experienced and responsible staff.

☐ Don't try to do everything yourself.

☐ Delegate various jobs and tasks and make your staff accountable for what they do.

☐ Use your time-chart religiously.

☐ Don't leave what should be done today for tomorrow.

☐ Make sure you always know what is going on in your salon and that you are in overall control.

☐ Take time off every week to relax and do things which you enjoy doing.

☐ Don't do business-related work or jobs in your time off.

From time to time everyone gets stressed, but it happens much more if you run your own business. Although we often talk about stress, we forget the very serious effect it has not only on our business but also on our personal lives and health. It has been proved that stress can kill.

Stress starts with tiredness, lack of sleep, irritation, lack of appetite for food and reduced libido. It increases the need for alcohol, cigarettes and caffeine. It strikes when 'things get on top of you', often due to:

- Bad time management.

- Excessive work load.

- Long hours.

- Not enough time for relaxation and social life.

- Not being able to 'get away from it all'.

ANGER MANAGEMENT

Anger is a complex phenomenon. Its roots can often go back to our childhood. Some of the factors that can contribute to anger include:

- Pressure (work, financial, relationship, etc.)

- Violation of one's privacy, space, beliefs or belongings

- Jealousy

- Rejection

- Frustration

- Lack of control

- Chaos

- Misunderstanding due to poor communication

When running your salon, there are times when everything goes wrong, everyone lets you down and everything that should not happen does happen. Your blood starts to boil and you began to lose it. *Stop. You cannot afford to 'lose it'.*

When you are in charge of people and a business, your anger and frustration must at all times be under complete control. There are two steps that you should follow:

1. ***Prevent anger.*** Before you get angry, your emotions get triggered by one or more of the above list. You will see it coming; try to block it. Good management skills generally prevent most of these, which in turn stops the development of anger.

2. ***Calm yourself if you do get angry*:** During an anger outburst, we temporarily lose the control of our speech and actions. Should you for any reason get angry, immediately think of the consequences of losing your temper, saying the wrong thing, and what reaction you might get. Take a deep breath and do and say nothing until you have calmed down and are in control of your actions and speech.

More often than not, what we say or do in anger is regretted later. So it is best not to say or do anything during an anger outburst. Those who suffer from regular and violent anger outbursts should seek psychological treatment.

STAFF MANAGEMENT

Your staff are probably the most important and enduring asset of your business, whether you employ just one or several. The difference between good and bad staff, apart from hassle and stress, can mean the success or failure of your business. As the majority of your clients will build up an empathetic relationship with your therapists, it is essential that your therapists are strong advocates of your beauty salon or you will always lose your good clients.

When you are starting your salon, if you are going to be a small operation with very limited finances, and if you are going to employ just one therapist, it is much better to have an experienced and responsible person than a junior. You will find that the junior will be of very limited use, resulting in you doing most of the work yourself, while an experienced therapist will share some of the responsibilities and will assist you with many of the tasks as well as doing treatments.

The secret of running any successful business is to employ the 'right people' and make good use of their skills and abilities. But you must train and manage them properly.

Employing well-trained and capable staff will cost more but you will reap the benefits in the long run. Always get your staff involved, motivated and rewarded for their performance. Training regularly is also essential as not only does it motivate them, it also keeps them interested in what they do, which ultimately keeps your clients happy and benefits your business.

Hold regular staff meetings, if possible once a week but at least once a month. Make sure your staff participate in discussions and suggestions and give feedback. Also, set weekly and monthly targets and incentives; it helps your staff's performance and will show who is interested in their work and who is not!

Make sure you develop a 'team spirit' in your salon. Your staff must work as a team and always help each other. There should be no place for a *loner* and no such thing as 'this is my work and that is your work'. Make your staff feel they are part of the business.

MONEY MANAGEMENT

Business is about making money, yet without money you can't start or run any business.

From day one you have to discipline yourself to respect and understand the value and importance of money. Learn what you can and should do with your money and what money can do for you.

In order to manage your money and finances properly, you must keep a good, clear, and uninterrupted record of all your financial transactions. This is something which should be done daily. Then your weekly and monthly accounting will become much simpler to handle and understand.

Your beauty business will have dozens of outgoings and only one source of income. Always remember, to make money, or profit, your total takings (money into business) must be greater than your total outgoings, or expenses (money out of business).

Keeping a clear and regular record will help you identify how your business is doing.

Spending your money wisely is essential to the profitability of your business. Spend where and when necessary, economise wherever and whenever you can but do not become a *penny pincher.*

Staying in control

Part of good management is to being in control (not to be mistaken for controlling people). In general, everything which needs to be managed needs some form of control. A good driver, for example, is always aware of his surroundings and is in control of his car, his actions and reactions on the road. We can say he is managing his driving well.

In your business, staff, quality, stock, cost, risk, money and time all need to be controlled.

Avoid becoming a 'control freak'. This will have a severe impact on your staff and your business.

STAFF CONTROL

Your staff need to be respected, motivated and to work in happy and friendly surroundings. However, their timekeeping, use of salon facilities and products, and behavior with customers must be monitored carefully.

QUALITY CONTROL

The quality of your treatments and service is of the utmost importance to your business as a beauty salon. You must make sure that consistent procedures and high-quality treatments are maintainedby all of your therapists. Regular surveys or questionnaires completed by your clients will help you to keep the quality of your treatments as high as possible.

STOCK CONTROL

Maintaining and knowing what stock you have and need is a must in every business. A regular stock control, at least once a month, is usually sufficient for a small salon.

However, sometimes you may need to check various stocks on a weekly basis if the turnaround is fast. This gives you a good idea of what is selling best and what is not. Too much or too little stock are both damaging to your income and cash flow. Stock control also allows you to notice if products are going missing.

COST CONTROL

This is often a difficult issue for people who are starting a new business. It is so easy to get carried away and let your costs run out of control. Remember, when you first start you are bound to be short of money, so every penny helps. Negotiate well, look for comparative prices, don't over-order, don't let enthusiastic salespeople persuade you into buying something that you don't need. Most importantly, continuously monitor your costs against your income. Your takings *must* always be greater than your outgoings.

RISK CONTROL

Running a business involves taking risks. The fact that you are going self employed and are opening a beauty salon means that you are prepared to take a risk. However, as long as you make informed decisions, taking into account all possibilities and alternatives, and have contingency plans in place to deal with them, then you are minimising your risk factor.

As an example, if you are going to buy expensive equipment, as long as you look at, say, three well-known makes, enquire about the companies and what after-sales service they offer, how long the machines have been in use, speak to people who have used them, and negotiate well for a competitive price, then your choice will more likely be a wise one and carry low risk.

FINANCIAL CONTROL

Financial control needs a certain amount of knowledge and experience. It is very important for you to know where your business is going financially. Again, this is one of those areas in which the majority of therapists have never been trained and can easily lead to disaster.

I will never forget meeting a beauty therapist who had recently bought a beauty salon as a going concern and had paid £80,000 for the business. She asked me if this was a good price. After asking her a few questions about the business, I was astonished to find out that, sadly, she did not know the difference between turnover and gross profit.

Understanding financial jargon and the basics of accounting is an important part of controlling your finances. A good accountant will always guide you on how your business is doing, but you still need to monitor the takings, the expenses and outgoings if you don't want things to get out of control.

TIME CONTROL

We have already discussed this very important aspect of your business under time management. Nonetheless, it is worth reiterating that if you don't control and manage your time, it will control you.

Using computers and the internet

The vast amount of information now available on the internet and the speed at which it can be obtained, processed and managed, makes a computer an essential tool in everyone's life and particularly in one's business, no matter how small or simple.

Apart from obtaining information, a simple computer programme can be used for keeping records and processing many daily operations. Some of the more useful operations are:

- □ Sending e-mails to customers

- □ Placing adverts

- □ Producing documents and writing letters

- □ Keeping accounts and calculating VAT

- □ Using spreadsheets to prepare cash-flow forecasts

- □ Calculating staff wages and tax and National Insurance deductions

- □ Maintaining stock levels

- □ Processing invoices, purchases and sales figures

- □ Storing clients' treatment records and data

- □ Keeping customer appointments in order

- □ Keeping staff records.

There are many software programmes specially designed to carry out specific functions. For example, you can buy a programme which will link your till to your computer and automatically take care of all your stock sales and availability, details of your customers, their treatments and appointments, and even send a text message to their mobile phone reminding them of their next appointment. Such programmes are extremely useful and will save you time in the day-to-day running of your salon. They will also remove some of the stress and worry associated with organising and managing your salon and without any doubt will improve the efficiency of your business.

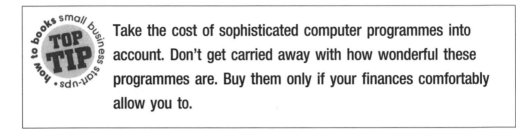

TOP TIP Take the cost of sophisticated computer programmes into account. Don't get carried away with how wonderful these programmes are. Buy them only if your finances comfortably allow you to.

Recession, credit crunch and difficult times

Everything which has an active element usually has a cycle. The economy of a country has cycles and goes through ups (periods of growth and expansion) and downs (periods of decline and downturn).

Most businesses follow this pattern, but if you are prepared for such changes and have good management in place, your business should be able to ride out a recession or downturn.

At the time of writing this book, our economy is in recession and is suffering as a result of what has become known as the credit crunch.

Hundreds of businesses are going bust every day. Factories and shops are closing down and those which can just about manage to stay afloat are laying off staff. Yet there are some which are producing good profits, taking advantage of the market and are expanding. These are companies, small or large, with good management, being well run with properly-controlled operations.

During recession and hard times – times which are often referred to as 'challenging and changing' – many manufacturers and supply companies reduce their prices and there are lots of offers around. Shops and premises become vacant and go on offer very cheaply. Unemployment usually rises, which means many people who have lost their jobs will be willing to work for less money. You can use all these to your advantage and operate and run your beauty business more profitably.

In business nothing stays still. You must move with the times and make necessary changes to adapt to the new conditions and economic circumstances. You could:

- ☐ Cut your costs and save wherever possible.

- ☐ Negotiate hard in your purchases.

- ☐ Look for deals from your suppliers.

- ☐ Look for alternative, possibly better and cheaper, suppliers.

- ☐ Improve the efficiency of your salon by better utilising your staff time.

- ☐ Identify non-profitable treatments and services and remove them.

- ☐ Cut staff hours and make therapists share job roles where possible.

- ☐ Continue marketing and advertising, promoting your salon and offering special deals.

- ☐ Look after your long-term and loyal clients.

You should NOT:

- ☐ Go crazy with price cuts. This will seriously damage your salon's image and will have a bad long-term effect.

- ☐ Cut corners or compromise the quality of your service or treatments.

The above lists don't just apply to bad times but should be part of your ongoing business operation. However, these actions do become more effective during a downturn when the economy is weak and people are cutting down on their spending.

When running your own business, you should always be positive and optimistic. When times are hard and business is difficult, think positive – it can only get better. As they say, it's all about confidence. If you believe in yourself, and feel and act confidently, then others around you will feel the same. You will then be in a better position to make sound judgements and better decisions, allowing you to get on the right road to achieving your goals.

9
FINANCE, MONEY AND ACCOUNTS

IN THIS CHAPTER

- ☐ Finding the finance for your salon

- ☐ Sources of finance

- ☐ How will clients pay?

- ☐ Keeping regular accounts

- ☐ Pricing services and products

- ☐ Tax, VAT, National Insurance and business insurance

In an ideal world it would be nice to have enough money to start your own salon without the need for any bank loans or borrowing. Unfortunately, more often than not, this is not the case and you will most probably need to borrow the money.

Financing your new business

In Chapter 2 we discussed various ways of starting your own beauty business, some of which would require little financing. However, to start a salon you will need tens of thousands of pounds, and apart from your own contribution the rest will have to be borrowed.

To fund your new beauty salon business, there are three things you have to establish:

1. How much capital do I need?

2. How long do I need to borrow it for?

3. Where should I go to raise it?

How much capital do I need?

In Chapter 7 we talked about your business plan, which includes the costing of your business. This is the total cost of everything you need to do, buy and pay for before you start your business and open your salon (start-up costs). Your cash-flow projection shows how much money you will need to keep the salon operating (running costs). Almost certainly, during the first few months your salon will not be self-sufficient and your budget must allow enough money to keep the business going until it becomes self-supporting.

If your projections and estimates of takings (the money the salon generates) are reasonably accurate, then as a rule-of-thumb, in your calculations you should allow enough money to pay your bills, purchases and wages for the first six months of your operation. This will ensure that your business is comfortably funded until it supports itself and starts to make a profit.

You can estimate the amount of money you will need to start your business by adding up the following:

- Cost of your shop
- Building work, renovation and decoration
- Professional, legal and licensing fees
- Registration and insurance fees
- Rent, rates, utilities and telephone bills
- Equipment, furniture and tools
- All other essentials such as accessories, uniforms, cleaning and toiletries
- Professional products and retail products
- Stationery and other related materials
- Marketing and advertising costs
- Wages
- Bank charges and interest.

The total sum of all the above costs, charges and fees less what funds you have available will be the amount of money you will need to raise.

For how long do I need to borrow?

This depends on how much money you are going to borrow, and how much money the business is going to have left after all bills and expenses are covered.

Example: If you borrow £30,000, your takings are £3,000 per week and your total outgoings are £2,000 per week, then you will have £1,000 left each week. Allowing for 8% compound interest per year, the total owed to the bank after three years will be approximately £37,800. If you now divide this by 3 × 52, your weekly repayment over three years will be approximately £242. This is well within your affordability and you will still have £758 left each week. It is wise to make sure that sufficient funds are left each week in the business for unexpected expenses.

How should I raise the money?

Family or Friends
Some people are lucky enough to be able to borrow from their families or from friends. With or without interest, this is the most convenient and probably the cheapest way of raising money for your salon.

They will often lend you the necessary money (invest in your business) without getting involved in the running of the business (usually called a sleeping partner or partners).

PARTNERSHIP
Another possibility for raising finance is to find an active partner who has the necessary funds available, and start the business together. In this case, the partner will be either another therapist working in the salon or someone with business experience who will get involved and share other tasks and responsibilities.

 Make sure you draw up an agreement between yourself and the person or people who lend you the money, and record everything that you have agreed, particularly the length of time for repaying the money.

BANK BORROWING
A bank loan or an overdraft facility is probably the most common and popular way of financing a new business. Most banks help, advise and provide finance for small businesses, often without any charge, to gain your custom.

Without any doubt, the first thing any bank will want from you is your business plan. If you have had an active account with the bank you are seeking finance from, it would be an advantage. As well as looking at your business plan, the bank will arrange an interview and will seek information about you and your business venture.

Before any bank will agree to a finance facility for your salon, it will have to seriously consider and be satisfied with your:

☐ Business plan

☐ Experience and skills in the field of beauty

☐ Employment and/or business track record

☐ Credibility and honesty

☐ Previous loan or borrowing history

☐ Existing bank account history

☐ Savings and your own financial contribution to the business

☐ Security put forward for the loan

☐ Personality

☐ Presentation skills in selling yourself and your business plan.

 Make sure you have a realistic business plan and are familiar with all aspects of it before you approach the bank.

 For your interview, you should be well and appropriately dressed, positive, optimistic and confident. The bank will be looking for a confident person with a realistic business plan.

OVERDRAFT

With this type of financing the bank will agree a maximum figure (a ceiling) that your account can operate within for a fixed period. Overdraft facilities are normally for short periods of one to two years and are subject to review at the end of the period. For example, if the bank agrees a £20,000 overdraft for one year, it will charge you an arrangement fee, and interest (a percentage over the base rate) only on the amount of the agreed overdraft that you use and the period that you use it. The more of the £20,000 facility you use and the longer you use it, the more interest you pay. The facility is available for you, but if you don't use it you won't be charged. For this reason, this is much more convenient but is more expensive to have.

This type of borrowing is best suited for a business when the finance need goes up and down and varies during the term of the facility. You will then pay interest only on the amount and time that you draw the money.

BANK LOAN

A business bank loan is generally for a longer term. The bank will agree a fixed amount for a fixed period at a fixed interest rate, usually a certain percentage over the base rate. This is invariably lower than that of an overdraft facility. Again, the bank will charge an arrangement fee to set up the loan for you. You will have to agree a fixed monthly repayment of the loan which will pay off the loan and its interest by the end of the term of the loan. The amount the bank will agree to lend you depends on your business plan. But generally speaking, the more money you put in, the larger the percentage of the amount you need to borrow will be offered to you. It is very rare that a bank will lend more than 50% of the total money required for a business.

Banks often require security against your business loan. The more security and the better the quality of your security, the larger the percentage of what you need will be offered to you. Banks prefer securities which can easily be converted into cash in case your business goes bust or you default on your repayments. Some common securities are a second charge over your property, endowment policies, bonds and shares.

Any security you offer against your loan, including your property, will be at risk if you don't keep up your repayments and you default on the terms and conditions of your loan.

Banks normally make their decision based on the risk factor of your business (prospect of making a good profit), your ability to run the business successfully (your experience in the field and your management skills) and the total amount you want to borrow as a percentage of your assets and securities.

Contrary to what most people believe, banks' interest charges and the terms of their loans are negotiable. If you have a good business plan, are confident about your proposals and what you are going to do, and have carefully thought about your beauty business in a realistic manner, then be shrewd and negotiate a deal that is suitable for you and not just good for the lender.

BANK ACCOUNT

Once your bank has agreed your financing requirements, they will open a current account for your business with cheque books and paying in books and will offer you a debit and cheque guarantee card. Try to agree a credit card for your business as well. It will make life a lot easier if you have one as some of your suppliers will insist on payment when you place your order.

Never mix your personal money and expenses with those of your business.

Your new business account will also be subject to various bank charges. For example, there will be a standard monthly operating charge, a percentage charged for depositing cash and a certain amount charged for every entry, such as cheques paid in, cheques drawn, direct debits, etc. By the end of the month all these charges can be quite significant. When you are opening your account, discuss all these with your bank and make sure you read and understand all the relevant terms and conditions. These are common to all banks and all business accounts.

Some banks offer free banking services to new businesses for a limited period (often the first year). Shop around to find the best deal.

Money

When your finances are arranged you will know exactly how much money you have available for your business. The major part of this money is for setting up the salon, and the rest for the running costs of the business during the first few months. Ensure that this part is not used as you will need it later.

By now you will have compiled a list of all the things you need to do and buy, and an estimate of how much money you have allowed for each one. This is your budget. It is most important that you stick to this and do not exceed it. Try to negotiate wherever and whenever possible, and if necessary look for alternatives. If you run out of money, it will be extremely difficult to borrow again so soon.

 It is very easy to become excited, get carried away and over-spend. If you can't afford it, don't buy it.

Although you will have an accountant to deal with all your accounts and taxes, it is essential that from day one you keep a clear and concise record of everything that you spend. Your records should include the date, the amount, how you have paid, and what the transaction was for. All of these should be supported by receipts.

 Don't keep records on bits of paper everywhere. Most stationery shops sell lined notebooks for this purpose. Buy and use one.

Client payments

Most of the salon's takings will be in credit card or debit card payments, with some cash and very occasional cheques. You will have little control over how people pay you for their treatments and purchases. Although we have previously discussed transactions in Chapter 3, because of their importance, we will once again point out the essential issues.

CREDIT CARDS

For your credit card takings you will need to register with one of the credit card companies such as Barclaycard (there are others run by NatWest and Lloyds) who will supply you with a terminal (a small electronic machine) and all the information that you will need to take payments by this method. You should then register with all other major card companies so that you can accept payments with their cards. The most commonly-used cards are Visa, Maestro, MasterCard, and American Express. Credit card companies will charge you a nominal percentage of the value of each transaction before they pay you. This charge *is* negotiable and usually depends on your turnover of each company's card (the amount that the company's card is used by your customers).

 You will be offered a much better rate of charges if you are a member of a beauty organisation such as The Guild of Beauty Therapists or BABTAC.

It is also essential that you have a separate telephone line for your credit card machine. This will then leave your salon telephone line free for your appointment calls. There is nothing worse for a client who wants to pay by credit card and leave the store promptly to be held up because you cannot take the payment as your telephone line is busy with an incoming call.

CHEQUES

Very few people pay by cheque these days and your salon will be no different. However, if you do get any, ask for the customer's cheque guarantee card and record the card number, the name, and the expiry date of the card on the back of the cheque. The maximum value of the cheque you can accept with some security is the value of the guarantee on the card. If the value of the cheque goes above the guarantee figure, the cheque will not be covered by the bank's guarantee policy. If the client does not have enough funds in the account the cheque will bounce and will be returned to you unpaid.

CASH

Although most people like the sound of cash, handling large quantities is inconvenient and also risky. Most banks charge businesses for cash which is deposited or taken out. Also, very few people carry a lot of cash around and most of your clients are unlikely to pay cash for big treatments or purchases. With regard to your salon purchases, never pay by cash if you can make your payments by other methods. Cash transactions are open to abuse and if things go wrong, you have less chance of any possible refunds or reimbursement of your money.

If your salon does take a lot of cash, make sure that you have sufficient insurance cover for the money in the salon as well as in transit to the bank. Don't let your cash takings accumulate. Bank them as soon as you can.

Petty cash and floats

Petty cash means small cash. It is a small amount of money, say £50 or so, kept in cash and used to pay for small everyday purchases, such as stamps, photocopying, tissue paper, etc. Each time you make a purchase, write a petty cash voucher and staple it to the receipt. At the end of the week, add all these together and enter the total figure into your cash book. You should then top up the petty cash box with enough money to bring it back to £50 (or whatever your original sum was).

 Use cash payments only for very small daily transactions and purchases such as milk or tissue paper or stationery. Charges against cheques and credit card payments outweigh their convenience when dealing in small amounts.

The float is the cash in your till at the start of the day. Every day you should start with the same amount. You should always make sure that you have a sufficient amount of mixed notes and coins in the till so that those who pay by cash can receive the correct change. The amount of float in the till will depend on your daily takings, but in most cases £50 is usually sufficient.

Security

All methods of payment are subject to fraud and abuse. With credit card transactions always make sure that you obtain authorisation while the customer is with you. You will be given full instructions on how to do this by your credit card company. Cheques must always be accepted only when accompanied with a cheque guarantee card, and details must be recorded on the back of the cheque. When taking cash, ensure that you are not confused by a potential fraudster. Always check £50 and £20 notes with an ultraviolet detector or special security pen to make sure that they are not fake.

Accounts

For effective management of your salon business, you will need to know and understand your accounts. That is, how much money is coming in, how much you are spending and paying out, how much you will need for later payments which are often quarterly (such as VAT, rent or insurance) and what is left after all of these.

And will you make any worthwhile profit from all the work and time that you put into your business.

For all this you will need a simple but effective accounting system which you can operate on a daily basis, and keep track of everything during the course of each week, month and year.

If your finances allow, a book-keeper can do all these tasks for you every week. Otherwise your accountant will advise you on how they would like you to keep various records so that it is simple enough for you to understand them and convenient for them to do the accounts at the end of each year.

Daily records

We have already discussed keeping daily takings records in Chapters 3 and 6. These figures, together with other sales and payments, need to be transferred into a format that your accountant can easily understand and use for accounts calculations.

Dividing your daily records into different sections will make your accounting system simpler.

1. Takings: all the payments made to your business, separating cash from other methods and clearly identifying those which are subject to VAT.

2. Expenditure: all your payments and purchases, indicating those with VAT.

3. Petty cash: all your small cash expenses.

4. Wages: these should have the name, amount and how it was paid, indicating all deductions such as tax and National Insurance.

5. Banking: all payments into and out of your bank account recorded in two separate columns.

You can keep these records in separate books or buy an accounts book (one very popular and easy-to-use book is EVRITE 707 which is sold in WHSmith and other stationery shops) which already has appropriate sections for each of the above. A petty cash book is normally kept separately.

Using these records, you can easily assess the financial state of your business every week. Your accountant will use them to do your VAT returns, and monthly and yearly accounts.

Keep all your till rolls and credit card transaction slips with your accounts book. Your accountant will need them for the yearly accounts calculations.

Expenditure

Your outgoings are either fixed costs (these are costs such as rent, rates and insurance which do not vary weekly or monthly regardless of how your business is doing) or variable costs (wages, electricity, product purchases, etc.). Variable costs will increase if you get busy and decrease if your salon is quiet.

When your accounts are done there will be many categories of outgoings and expenses, but for ease of understanding you can classify them under five headings:

- ☐ Wages

- ☐ Stock and product purchase

- ☐ Fixed charges

- ☐ Interest and bank charges

- ☐ Others

This list should also be used when you are writing a cash-flow forecast which will give you an instant overview of your salon's financial state.

At the end of each week, use your recorded daily figures and add them all up to find out what sort of week your salon has had. By monitoring and knowing how things are going on a weekly basis, you can take appropriate corrective action.

Salon takings

Variations in daily takings are not very significant and should not cause you any worry. It is quite normal for your business to be very busy one day and absolutely dead another. All sorts of factors can create such a variation. However, your weekly and monthly takings should be taken very seriously. You should regularly monitor and compare them with previous weeks' and months' takings and those of comparable periods in previous years. For example, you should compare Easter week of one year with Easter week of the previous year. This will easily indicate whether your business has moved forwards, backwards or has remained the same.

After a while, a pattern should develop showing your salon's busiest periods, the times when your business is steady and when in the week, month or year your salon is quieter. This knowledge is extremely useful and gives you a good insight into your business. It will help you to:

☐ Plan for your own and your staff's holidays.

☐ Increase or decrease your stock.

☐ Increase or reduce the number of staff and their working hours.

☐ Vary your opening days and hours.

 It is a good idea to keep the records of your treatment takings separate from product sales. This will enable you to monitor and assess each part of the business separately.

 Having up-to-date knowledge of your salon's takings and outgoings gives you the necessary information to make sensible commercial decisions and be in control of what is happening with your business.

Pricing

The prices you charge for your services, treatments and products play an extremely important role in the success of your business. If you price too high, you may not get the trade; if you price too low, you will not make enough profit and your business might go bust. Unless your product, service or treatment is completely new and unique, the market has itself established an acceptable price range for most treatments within which all salons operate.

To produce your price list for your salon within this range, take into account:

☐ Where your salon is located.

☐ Your fixed expenditure.

☐ What your competitors around you charge.

☐ What type of market you are aiming at.

☐ The time taken to do the treatment.

☐ How much product will be used for each treatment.

☐ How much skill, training and experience are needed to carry out the treatment.

☐ What hourly rate of charges will cover *all* your expenses, including taxes, and leave you with an acceptable profit.

As an example, let's take the price of a manicure. If your salon is in the expensive area of Belgravia in London, your fixed expenditure will be quite high and your competitors will be charging the higher end of the market prices. If you have decided to go for such an upmarket salon, pampering your clients and giving them all the time that they want, then your price should reflect this; be competitive with the competition and within 5% of what they charge.

However, if you have decided to cater for the busy career person who is always short of time, wants a good manicure but wants to just walk in without an appointment and get it done quickly, then you can easily charge 15–20% lower than your immediate competition. This reduction is compensated for by the fact that you will do the treatment in less time.

On the other hand, if your salon is located in a small town, your fixed expenditure will be much lower, any possible competitor will be charging lower prices, and unless you are aiming for a very upmarket salon, when fixing your prices you should consider what the people of that town are prepared to pay. This will probably be about 30% lower than that of the previous example in Belgravia.

If a treatment requires a specific skill, training or qualification, and needs specific insurance, then the price charged will be much higher than a normal treatment (comparing hour with hour). IPL and laser are good examples of such treatments.

A salon might charge £40 per hour for treatment in a small town, about £65 per hour in some areas of London and maybe £100 to £120 per hour in the more exclusive parts.

Tax, VAT and National Insurance

Unless you have decided to do everything yourself, which is not recommended, your accountant will look after the various taxes and National Insurance. However, a basic understanding of them is very useful and at times necessary.

TAX

As a self-employed person, your business taxes are calculated and paid on a yearly basis. When your tax year ends, your accountant will take all your account books, receipts, bank statements, cheque books, paying in books, invoices, etc. and will prepare your business account for the year.

If you are also on the payroll and receive wages, together with all your staff, you will also have to pay income tax which is deductable every time you are paid, weekly or monthly. Again, unless you are going to do the wages yourself, which is not advisable, your book-keeper or accountant will do all the calculations and tell you how much everyone should be paid.

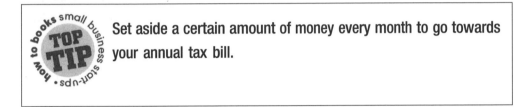

Set aside a certain amount of money every month to go towards your annual tax bill.

The amount of tax your business will have to pay will depend on how well your salon has performed during the year and how your business is registered. Since your VAT is calculated and paid quarterly, from your VAT figures you should be able to calculate your estimated profit or loss for that quarter (your total income less all your expenses and outgoings is roughly your gross profit). Throughout the year this will give you a pretty good idea of what your profit or loss for the year might be.

Having a good accountant who will advise you on all your accounts and tax affairs is a worthwhile investment in your business. The accountant's fees are often offset by the saving they make in your money and your time.

Sometimes it is better to have one accountant do all your accounts as well as wages and VAT returns. In some cases you may find it cheaper to have a book-keeper doing your wages and VAT, while the accountant does the yearly accounts. Find out which is more economical for you.

VAT

Value Added Tax (VAT) is a tax that is paid on purchases of goods and services, and collected on sales of goods or services. It is operated throughout the European Union (EU), including the United Kingdom. It applies to all businesses when their turnover exceeds a certain level, which is fixed in the annual budget by the government. Your accountant will advise you of this figure and you must register immediately if you qualify.

Once you are registered, you must follow the guidelines and regulations very carefully as not all products and services are subject to the same rate of VAT. There are the *zero rate*, *reduced rates* and the *standard rate*. You will have to apply the correct VAT rate to all your prices and charge your customers accordingly. The VAT that you have been charged on your purchases and expenses will then be reclaimable.

The amount of VAT you charge less the amount you have been charged is what you have to pay back to HM Revenue and Customs every quarter. This process is known as preparing your VAT Return. The Revenue takes this extremely seriously and for this reason it is advisable to have a book-keeper or to arrange for your accountant to do your VAT Returns for you.

The VAT on goods and services that you supply is known as your output tax and the VAT on all the purchases and services you receive is called your input tax.

Example: If you buy a product for £30 inclusive of VAT, to work out the net price (price without VAT), assuming a VAT rate of 17.5%:

Divide £30 by 1.175, which gives £25.53.

If the VAT rate is 15%, divide by 1.150; if the VAT rate is 20%, divide by 1.120; and so on.

Example: If a product is £12 net of VAT, then the VAT will be £12 × 17.5% = £2.10 (at a rate of 17.5%).

Example: If you buy a product for £10 and the applicable VAT rate is 17.5%, and assuming that your selling margin is 40%, then your retail selling price will be calculated as follows:

£10 + (£10 × 40%) = £14. Net of VAT
VAT will be 17.5% × 14 = £2.45
Add this VAT to your net selling price: £14 + £2.45 = £16.45. This is your retail price. The £2.45 which is the VAT will be paid to HM Revenue and Customs.

Government websites offer a lot of useful information. For VAT matters, visit www.hmrc.gov.uk/vat

NATIONAL INSURANCE CONTRIBUTION

National Insurance contributions are another payment that you have to be aware of when running a business and employing staff. Depending on whether you register your salon as a limited company, partnership or sole trader, your National Insurance contributions will fall into different categories. Once again, your accountant will advise you on all these and when wages are calculated the correct deductions will be made.

Accounts, wages, VAT and NIC are specialist subjects and unless you are fully qualified it is best to leave them all to your accountant. Your business will be better off by you spending your time managing your staff and the salon.

Insurance

Your premises, your business, your therapists and other staff all need insurance, not only for your peace of mind but sometimes as a requirement by law.

Unless you own your shop outright, your landlord normally insures the building and passes on your proportion to you.

Your business should have adequate insurance to cover all your stock, equipment and furniture, money in the till and in transit, loss of business income and profit, employer's liability, legal expenses and tax enquiry cover. Insurance companies often offer special schemes for beauty salons which cover everything you need.

All insurance companies will require a business intruder alarm system which is installed and maintained by a company acceptable to the local police and is a member of UKAS (United Kingdom Accreditation Services) and satisfies British standard BS4737 or European standard EN50131. Make sure you have an alarm installed.

You and all your staff also need treatment insurance cover. This is an insurance cover for treatment risk liability and public/products liability.

 A reputable and specialist insurance broker will be able to arrange all your insurance needs. Membership of BABTAC (British Association of Beauty Therapy and Cosmetology) offers comprehensive block insurance schemes which are tailor-made for beauty salons and offered at a discounted price.

 With all your insurance policies, make sure that you read all the documents and the small print thoroughly and are satisfied with the cover offered to you before you accept and pay. Never be under-insured.

10
MARKETING, ADVERTISING AND PROMOTION

IN THIS CHAPTER

☐ Where is your market?

☐ Who are your market?

☐ What does your market want?

☐ How do I get to my market?

☐ How should I attract my market?

We often use the words 'advertising' and 'marketing' without fully appreciating their impact on our business.

The word 'marketing' is derived from 'market', which is basically a collection or group of people who are available for a service, transaction or purchase of a product. Without a market there is no sale or purchase or service and there will be no business. For a service, such as your beauty salon, you also need a market (your customers) – without them you will have no business!

It is therefore very important to identify the market (the type of clients who are going to come to your salon, buy your products, and use your services and treatments) and then ensure that you create a market (get customers coming to you) for your business. This is known as 'marketing'.

Getting your marketing right is crucial to the success of your business. You should create a clear marketing strategy that will help you identify potential customers and then target them with appropriate products and treatments.

Identifying your market

When you are planning to start your own salon, you will be considering the following:

☐ Looking for premises.

☐ Researching different areas.

☐ Checking the size of the market in each area.

☐ Looking at various equipment and products.

☐ Checking your competition in the area.

☐ Deciding on your choice of treatments and prices.

☐ Interviewing therapists.

☐ Collecting all sorts of other information.

In all these areas, you will be doing what is known as market research. By analysing your market research information, you will be in a position to produce your marketing plan, which itself will be part of your business plan. Large organisations usually use market research agencies that specialise in this type of work. Small businesses cannot afford such agencies' fees and tend to do their own research.

 Radio interviews, TV programmes, newspaper articles and some websites often have information which will be of immense use to you. When you see, hear or read them, write down and use this information.

Marketing

Marketing is knowing who your clients are, what they want, and you providing it for them, when they want it, at a price that is acceptable to them and profitable to your business.

Marketing and market research is not a one-off activity. It should be a continuous part of your business operation. Your marketing strategy will allow you and your business to be prepared for and adapt to changes in conditions, fashion, the economic climate and clients' needs.

As part of your market research, you should always be aware of and continuously monitor:

☐ Your customers' requirements

☐ Their main treatments

☐ The most popular hours of the day

☐ Your busiest days of the week

☐ Your busiest months of the year

☐ The number of times treatments are given each week or month

☐ The best-selling products

☐ The comings and goings of competitors in your area

☐ Your competitors' treatments and prices

☐ Other activities in the area which might affect your business.

All the above information, when analysed, will clearly show you:

1. How your business is performing.

2. How it is likely to perform in the future.

3. How these factors are likely to affect your business.

This will help you in your decisions and the running of your salon, and ultimately improve the operation and success of your business.

Information is vital in business. The more information you have and use, the better you can see where your business is going and take the correct business decisions.

To put something right, you must know what has gone wrong. And to know what has gone wrong, you need information. So listen to everything you can hear, watch everything you can see, and keep a record of everything that happens.

The above list should also be extended to cover your staff and your suppliers. For example, you should monitor and know the following:

☐ Which therapists are the most popular.

☐ Which ones are often late or have excessive time off.

☐ Who sells most products and who does not make any effort.

☐ Which of your suppliers have the best delivery record.

☐ Which ones have good advertising campaigns and provide you with posters and samples.

☐ Who has good back-up support and gives best payment terms.

Once you have identified your market, you must make sure you produce a market for your service or product. In a beauty salon, we know generally what our clients want. Your salon's role will be to provide the treatments and products that they want, when they want them, at a price which is right for them *and* your business.

 Once your business is up and running, one of the best ways of doing market research is by giving your clients a simple questionnaire asking questions about your staff, your salon and their treatments and inviting them to comment on anything else they wish.

 Talking and listening to your clientèle is a good source of obtaining information for your market research.

Creating your market

Just having a good business idea or opening a glamorous salon will not alone guarantee a successful business.

Once you have selected the location of your salon you need to make sure that you create a market for it. The following are some of the factors which will affect the creation of a good market for your beauty salon.

COMPETITION

When you are establishing a business, whatever the service or product, and you want to find out your market, you must seriously consider what competition you will have and who your competitors are. This will help you in deciding on several important issues such as the choice of treatments, products you will stock, hours of opening and even the choice of décor and colour scheme.

 If you find out that there is no beauty salon in the area, find out why. It is possible that there is no market for it.

LOCATION

Depending on the area, your clients' needs will vary. Make sure you offer what is popular and in demand in the area. For example, in a city centre where most of your potential clients are office workers, very few will have time for long relaxing treatments during the working day. Most of what they have will be short and fast treatments such as waxing or manicure/pedicure.

 **Make sure your treatments and products are compatible with the location. For example, spray tanning is more in demand by younger clients while facials are probably more popular among older clients.**

QUALITY OF TREATMENT

This is quite obvious. The higher the quality and experience of your staff, the better the quality of your offered treatments. This will automatically attract the type of clients who expect a bit extra and will be prepared to pay more.

YOUR STAFF

The quality and experience of your staff and therapists will be a major factor in the type of business you run, the clientèle it attracts and its ultimate success. This subject was discussed in Chapter 5, and its importance must not be underestimated.

PRICING

Pricing your treatments and products was discussed in Chapter 9. However, as it is vitally important to have the right price for each service, we will look again at these important issues.

The location of your salon will be a major factor in deciding your pricing. If your salon is in the heart of London's Mayfair your pricing will be totally different from a salon in a small town in the country. This is simply because your rent, rates, wages, insurance and service changes will all be much higher in one than the other.

Another factor is the amount of competition and the nature of their services. If there are no other beauty salons nearby, you are in a more advantageous position than if there are one or two others close by offering the same treatments as you.

The products you use will affect the cost of your treatments. For example, if you use a cheap and unknown brand of tanning spray, then you will have to charge less than if you use a better and well-known brand such as St Tropez, which will cost you more to buy.

 **Don't price yourself out of the market. But remember that by being cheap you will not necessarily attract more customers and could ruin your business.** *The price has to be right to attract customers and for the business to make profit.*

You can now see that the location of your salon, choice of treatments and products, quality of treatments, selection of your therapists and staff, your prices, as well as the décor and overall atmosphere of your salon will all contribute to create a market for your business. This market is what your salon will depend on for its success and profitability.

This is when you have to decide if your salon is going to be basic (cheap and cheerful), middle of the road (medium range of prices) or upmarket (very high quality and high prices).

Once you have decided which one of these options you want your beauty salon to be, you can start your marketing, develop your market accordingly and establish your salon.

Advertising

Advertising is the process of making people aware of your business, its services and products, and persuading them to come to you and rather than to your competition. In other words, it creates an awareness and desire among your existing and potential market. The more effective your advertising, the bigger and wider your market becomes.

The benefits of advertising vary enormously and depend on many factors. The following is a list of methods:

☐ **Radio:** Local radio is an excellent way of advertising but can be quite costly. If you can manage to get an interview on the radio to talk about your salon and the treatments you offer, that will be free.

☐ **Local newspapers:** Adverts in local papers reach a wide range of people and businesses and are effective. They are much cheaper than a radio advert.

☐ **Leaflets:** Also known as a mail-shot, this is a good method of reaching a particular area or a selected group of people. The leaflets can be individually delivered or be part of another delivery, making it cheaper to distribute. Also, compared with a newspaper advert you have a lot more room to express what you want to say and even include a picture. The Royal Mail has very effective distribution packages.

☐ **Posters:** You can have your own posters printed and displayed in either your window or on a billboard outside your salon. Most product suppliers provide advertising posters free. Ask for them and display them.

☐ **Business card:** This is a must. It should carry the name of your business, your logo, address and telephone number, and your website address. It is useful to give cards out in meetings to potential customers, and also use them for writing the client's appointment time and date.

☐ **Open Day:** You can allocate a day or an evening when your salon will be open to everyone for a free demonstration of a product or treatment, with free samples and possibly a drink and some nibbles. Invite potential customers and tell others about the event. It works wonders.

☐ **Advertorial:** An advertorial is an article written in a newspaper or magazine about your salon or a treatment at your salon, without any cost to you. This is normally arranged with the editor of the publication who experiences the treatment or product from you free of charge and then writes the article about it. To get this, you have to contact the editor of the publication and discuss the product or treatment that you want to be written about.

☐ **Trade journals:** Generally expensive, but quite effective if they are used for special occasions, special offers or announcing a new treatment.

☐ **PR agencies:** Public relations agencies (PR) have a lot of contacts in the right places and can promote your business very effectively. However, their fees are normally very high and will become cost effective only if you have several salons.

☐ **Website:** A Website is a *must* for your beauty salon. Your website will have clear information about your salon, the products you sell and the treatments you offer. It will also tell your potential customers where you are located, your opening hours and everything else you want them to know. It will cost you only once to have it made for you and a very small amount yearly to maintain it. It is well worth investing in a good website. For our salon we have used www.zfdesigns.com

☐ **Internet sites:** Internet directories such as Yell.com offer packages for a yearly fee and are an excellent way of exposing your salon and reaching potential clients.

☐ **E-mail:** The cheapest and fastest method of reaching potential or existing customers is by e-mailing them. Details of new products, new treatments, special offers or selected discounts can be sent to your existing clientèle, potential new customers or local businesses and companies. This is a free service, it's fast, and can be personalised.

☐ **Point of sale:** A product or a small poster near the till where customers pay often encourages the impulse buyer to make a purchase, ask about the treatment you are displaying or make an appointment.

☐ **Printed bags:** Many salons use bags printed with their name and logo. This is also a good way of sending your customers out with something to remember you by. However, unless you use and print a large quantity, the bags can be costly.

☐ **Word of mouth:** Clients pleased with their treatments will always talk and spread the news about your salon and your staff. This is great and absolutely free. But remember that dissatisfied customers will also talk.

☐ **Recommendation:** This is a by-product of word of mouth and it feels good to get clients who have been recommended. It's like getting a prize for your good work or service. Word of mouth and recommendations are probably the best and most powerful methods of gaining customers.

When you place a series of adverts, always use your logo and stick to a brand format but change the wording. This gives the reader variety, but creates familiarity with your company's name and logo.

Advertising companies, newspapers and magazines use shrewd and persistent salespeople. Don't be forced to buy an advert you don't want. If you do decide to place an advert, negotiate and bargain hard as their prices can often come down substantially. They work on large margins.

It is clear that every business will benefit to some degree from one form or another of advertising. It is the method, content and timing which will make the difference in the results you get. When you decide to advertise you should design and write your advert so that:

☐ Your existing clients are reminded of any new products, treatments and offers.

☐ Potential new clients are made aware of who you are, where your salon is, and what you offer, and why they should use your treatments and your salon rather than others.

Any benefit gained from your advertising will increase your client numbers, which will in turn help your business to grow.

Good advertising is more cost-effective in the early days of the business than when the salon is established. Recommendation plays a much more important role in gaining new customers when the salon is up and running.

You can have the best product and service in the world, but unless the market hears and knows about it and is made aware of where and when it is offered, nothing will happen.

Timing of your advertising is also very important. Special offers and promotions often give better results just before a special occasion or a season such as Christmas, Valentine's Day, Mother's Day or Easter.

 When you write your advert, make sure your message is simple, clear and short. And don't forget your business's contact details.

Many people who start their own business get excited and carried away with fancy advertising. They often get persuaded by advertising companies to take expensive adverts in famous and national magazines. Although this may be good for big national companies, it will have very little benefit to a small local salon. Stick to your local market and target your potential customers directly, particularly in the early days.

Promotions

From time to time you should have special offers and promotions. These should be well timed and very occasional. The main purpose of short-period offers and promotions is to do the following:

- ☐ Introduce a new product.

- ☐ Introduce a new treatment.

- ☐ Boost the sale of a particular service or product.

- ☐ Attract customers at certain times of the day or week.

- ☐ Attract new clients.

- ☐ Increase your takings and cash flow.

You can make up your own offers and promotional ideas to suit your salon and clientèle. Some of the most commonly used ideas for promotions are as follows:

☐ Buy one product get one free, or get a second one half price.

☐ Have one treatment and get your second one half price.

☐ Book and pay for a course of treatments (say five) and get the sixth one free.

☐ Have two treatments on the same visit and get 10% off.

☐ Introduce a friend for a treatment and get your own treatment (the same) half price.

☐ 10% off certain lines of products or treatments for a week or a fixed period.

☐ Offer of the week; for example, a free manicure with every facial treatment.

☐ 10% off all treatments before 12p.m.

☐ Half-price treatments for senior citizens on Mondays (or your most quiet day).

If promotions become ongoing, clients will get used to them and expect them all the time, defeating the whole purpose and resulting in lower revenue.

LOYALTY AND DISCOUNT CARDS

Some businesses produce loyalty cards and give them to their regular clients. These cards encourage clients to stick with your business in order to either get their points, discount or their free treatment, depending on what your card offers. As a form of encouragement, they can also be issued to larger local offices and companies where word of mouth recommendation is common. Some cards are designed to offer a flat rate of discount; others collect points with a very small nominal value which can later be exchanged for goods or treatment. Some will record the number of treatments or purchases (say five or six) and then give one free. These cards are quite popular and are well worth considering.

11
FORMULA FOR SUCCESS

IN THIS CHAPTER

- ☐ What is the You Factor?

- ☐ Do I have the You Factor?

- ☐ How to sell

- ☐ How to negotiate

- ☐ The dos and don'ts for a successful salon

- ☐ Keeping clients 'in love' with your salon

In previous chapters we have outlined the necessary steps to starting, running and managing a beauty salon. The big question now is, 'Will everyone who follows these guidelines be successful?' The answer is yes but to different degrees. The level of success and how long it takes to become successful will depend on one other very important factor – **YOU**.

The You Factor

Let us assume two people start identical businesses, next to each other, on the same day, with the same interior and exterior designs and layout, matching colour scheme, using the same equipment, the same treatments and price lists, employing the same number of therapists with identical qualifications, experience and skills. And let us also assume that they both follow all the dos and don'ts of this book. After six months one salon is doing better than the other. The reason for this is the 'You Factor' of the person running the business.

If you study successful entrepreneurs, business people and world leaders, the people who have made an impact, people like Winston Churchill and Richard Branson, you will see that their success and achievements cannot be boiled down to one or two factors. These people can very rarely give one or two reasons for their success. What has made them what they are is their You factor.

It is almost impossible to describe the You Factor; it is a complex phenomenon which is unique to every person and although it can be greatly influenced, it cannot be completely altered.

The following attributes when combined will form the You Factor of a person.

PERSONALITY

The personality of a person can be defined as a set of characteristics unique to that person, which influence and affect that person's behaviour in different situations.

ATTITUDE

Attitude can be positive or negative and describes a person's degree of like or dislike for someone, some place, some event or some thing (this can be absolutely anything; colour, smell, food, religion, holiday, cat, work, etc.). A person's attitude is a kind of judgement and is normally the result of either direct experience or observation. Some theories believe that indirect hereditary variables may affect a person's attitude. It is also believed that because attitude can be formed from experience, it can be changed with new experiences as well as by persuasion.

CHARISMA

The word 'charisma' originates from the Greek word 'kharisma' which means 'gift of God'. It is meant to describe a person's unique personal charm, magnetism and appeal. It is the ability to inspire, lead, charm, persuade or influence other people.

KNOWLEDGE

Knowledge can be defined as the understanding and learning of a skill or subject through experience or education. You have knowledge of something if you can use it, explain it or do it. If you gain a vast amount of knowledge about a particular subject, you will be classified as an expert or authority in that field.

INFORMATION

Information is closely related to concepts such as knowledge, instruction, communication and representation. It can be defined as a message which is received and understood. Information is knowledge gained through experience, study or instruction.

Information is always *about* something (people, places, size, colour or weight, an event or a feeling, even a sound). Information is not always accurate and can be a truth or a lie, but it is still information.

During a decision-making process, the more information you have the better your judgement will be and, the better the decision you make.

POSITIVITY

This is how positive a person is. It is accepted that people who are positive look on the bright side of life, are optimists, and believe in good things. They always see a light at the end of the tunnel. The opposite of being positive is being negative. These people see the bad and ugly side in everything, are often pessimists and can think only negatively.

The best example is the classic glass with half water. The positive person will say the glass is half full, while the negative person will argue that the glass is half empty. They are of course both right. The only difference is that the positive person will enjoy the half glass of water, while the negative person will be miserable believing that his glass is half empty.

CONFIDENCE

Confidence can be explained as a state of being certain of the outcome of something. If a person has confidence in himself or herself, then that person is said to have self-confidence. A person with strong self-confidence does not believe in failure, enjoys the situation that he or she is involved in and is always positive. This is simply because there will be much less worry about negative consequences and as a result the concentration is focused on a positive and successful outcome. People with confidence are normally good communicators, or can easily learn the skill of communication.

Politicians, teachers, actors and actresses, salespersons, reporters and, sadly, con-people generally have a very high level of self-confidence and are very good communicators. They enjoy the benefits of these two attributes in their daily work.

People with a high level of self-confidence often possess and show a certain degree of arrogance and superiority which, if not controlled, can sometimes have an adverse effect on other people.

SELF-BELIEF

Being confident gives a person a sense of self-belief. Self-belief can be described as being certain of coping with a situation, whatever the outcome. Such a person believes in what they say or do, and will strongly defend their opinion, decision or conviction.

AMBITION

Ambition can be described as the desire and motivation to gain power, wealth or fame, or reach a specific goal or set of goals in life. Both ambition and aspiration can be nurtured from childhood, but it is believed that often something in our life acts as a trigger for them.

COMMITMENT

Commitment is a pledge, strong obligation, self-promise, act of duty or feeling of loyalty to someone or something and can be mental, social, physical, financial or personal. A person with commitment will do everything in their power and ability to show or prove their loyalty.

CHARACTER

The character of a person can be described as a combination of their qualities, features, behaviour, abilities and attributes. This is what distinguishes one person from another. A person with strong character is often more persuasive and determined in what they say and do.

COMMUNICATION

To communicate is to be able to pass information from one source to another. This information can be one's knowledge, ideas, views, thoughts, opinions or feelings. A good communicator is a person who can transfer his or her information to his or her recipient easily and smoothly and similarly receives theirs. When we communicate with other people there are three elements in our communication:

1. The words we use – **what** we say.

2. The tone of our voice – **how** we say it.

3. Our facial movement – **body language**.

It is believed that during verbal face-to-face communication the impact is made up of 50% body language, 40% tone of voice and only 10% the content of what we say.

Having good communication skills is essential when managing people and staff. This is one of those attributes of the You Factor that can be learned. There are numerous books, courses and seminars teaching us how to be good communicators – it pays dividends to use them. Because of the importance of this subject, communication and its effect on clients has already been discussed in Chapter 6.

ABILITY TO MANAGE

Although we have already discussed the importance of management in Chapter 8, it is useful to see its relevance to the You Factor here.

Management is all about planning, organising and controlling, be it something or someone.

In a business sense, a good definition of 'ability to manage' is the ability to organise, co-ordinate and monitor the activities and performance of the business and the people involved, in accordance with certain objectives and policies, to achieve the goals and objectives of the business.

Management skills are imperative to the success of your business and can be learned from many publications and by attending management courses and seminars.

The ability to manage is a big contributor to your You Factor.

Analysing your own You Factor

Some of the above attributes are part of our makeup from birth, some we learn and develop through our life experience, and a few can be developed and changed by training.

By recognising and acknowledging these attributes you can change and adapt the way you approach every aspect of your life. Then, by improving and strengthening the weak attributes and incorporating the missing ones, you can alter your own You Factor and pave the way for success.

It is important that you make an assessment of your various attributes by realising your strengths and weaknesses. This will help you realise how your natural capabilities can be used effectively in your business.

A good way to assess the above attributes is to score each one (almost as if you were applying for and a job). Draw a table comprising three columns (low, medium and high) and put a cross in the relevant column for each attribute. Then look at the Low (Weak) and Medium (Average) columns and using examples relating to real life, write down an account or story to demonstrate each one.

The following table shows a hypothetical example.

	Low (Weak)	Medium (Average)	High (Strong)
Personality			X
Attitude		X	
Charisma			X
Knowledge		X	
Information		X	
Positivity			X
Confidence	X		
Self-belief	X		
Ambition			X
Commitment			X
Character		X	
Communication		X	
Ability to manage		X	

Example:

Let us take 'Ability to manage', which has a cross under Medium (Average). You may write the following:

'I was in charge of a team of six people in my previous job role and I managed to inspire them and bring out the best in them.'

This example and the account given demonstrate that this person has a reasonably good ability to manage but there is room for improvement.

The column with 'Confidence' is marked Low (Weak), which is not good. You may write the following:

'I get very nervous when I have to discuss or negotiate the price of something; I would rather just pay what I am told.'

This person must take every action to improve and boost their confidence as it is essential in running a salon.

If you follow this exercise, it will help you identify your strengths and weaknesses and enable you to take the necessary steps to address them.

Selling and negotiating

Although running a beauty salon will not need you to be a salesperson, the ability to 'sell' your ideas behind various treatments, the products, your promotions and even your suggestions and ideas to your staff, will be necessary and to your advantage.

Some people are born natural salespeople, others get training and become good in selling. Some just hate the thought of trying to sell to someone and get very embarrassed. If you are a good communicator and enjoy selling, you have an advantage. If you are not, then you would be well advised to learn the basics of selling techniques and by continuous practice improve this very useful skill. The ability to sell and negotiate is something that you will get better at with practice and time. The ability to sell and negotiate is very useful in everyday life but almost essential in business.

 Using recognised sales techniques will help you turn a small interest in your product or treatment into a sale or future regular custom.

The majority of your retail products will probably support your beauty treatments and act as follow-ups or be used between treatments. A client who has just had a treatment done and is pleased, is very likely to make an appointment for the next treatment or even book and pay for a discounted course of treatments. If recommended, your customer is also likely to buy a product which will boost the benefits of the treatment. All of these will require a bit of selling which, if successful, will increase your takings and improve your cash flow.

THE ART OF SELLING

Your clients and customers can be divided into three groups:

1. Those wanting to make a purchase or have treatment. They have already made up their mind and decided what they want, and they will have it regardless.

2. Those making an enquiry.

3. Those who are not so sure of what they want and come in to ask questions, and talk about various treatments and products.

Group 1 customers have already made their enquiries, checked the price, know exactly what they want and may also have made their appointment.

Group 2 are enquirers and information collectors. They have no intention of buying or having anything done during that visit. But, depending on how they have been treated, they may become customers in the future.

Those in group 3 are the majority of people who visit your business. They need information and should be well looked after. They have come for advice from you, the professional, and should be told the benefits of your product or service (treatment in a salon's case) and then be convinced and persuaded that while they are there it is the right time to buy or have a treatment. They need to be sold to.

 Every time a person comes to your salon, a sale and a purchase take place. Either you sell them a treatment or product (they buy your product or service) or you buy their excuse for not purchasing anything (they sell you their excuse).

The following suggestions will make selling easier and more successful:

☐ Make sure that you know all about your product or treatment before you try to sell it. This includes what it is, what it does and the benefit to the customer, and **what it costs**.

☐ Make your customer feel good and gain their trust.

☐ Never be forceful; gentle recommendation works better.

☐ Ensure that your customer is told and knows exactly what they are getting and what it is going to cost them.

☐ Don't try to be 'clever'. Most people will see right through you.

☐ Be honest and sincere; don't try to sell something that the customer does not need.

☐ Always clearly explain to the customer the features (what it is), the action (what it does, or is good for) and the benefit (what benefit it has for the customer) of your product or treatment.

☐ For a sale to take place when you want it to, four ingredients are necessary:

– **Need:** You should make sure that what you are offering your customer is what they need. If they have absolutely no need for something, it is very unlikely that they will buy it or have it done, unless you are an extremely experienced and professional salesperson. By asking as many questions as possible you can find out why they have come to your salon and what they really need. Once you know this, you know which is the right product or treatment to offer.

– **Desire:** A customer is very unlikely to buy something or agree to a treatment unless they have a desire for it. This is something that a good salesperson can develop by giving the customer as much information as possible and making sure they are told about the features and benefits of what you are trying to sell.

– **Urgency:** If you create a sense of urgency, you are much more likely to sell your product or treatment right away. Urgency can be developed by having items or treatments on offer for a limited time, or the availability of a therapist there and then for an immediate treatment.

– **Affordability:** Ensure that what you are offering is at the right price for the customer and that they are likely to be able to afford it. You can ask questions like, 'Do you have a budget for this treatment or product?', especially if they are buying a gift for someone else. Offer them any promotion you may have or any discount you can give. Give them all the information about alternatives. Before you finalise any sale, make sure that the customer is happy with the price and that they can afford it. They should want to make the purchase or have the treatment – if not, give them encouragement.

☐ Ask your customer questions to which the answer is in agreement with what you have said. This will get you a commitment from them which will help towards a decision to purchase.

☐ Some people can never decide. After you have found out their needs and likes/dislikes, and price level, you may have to make the decision for them.

Good salespeople are generally confident people with good communication skills. We talked about both these skills earlier and they are both attributes of the You Factor which can be gained and improved by training.

If you want to be good in selling, make sure that you have confidence in yourself and that you can communicate well.

NEGOTIATION

Negotiating, or bartering as it used to be known, has been a common practice for thousands of years in many countries in Asia, Africa and southern Europe. In central and northern Europe, including the United Kingdom, people have not been used to negotiating and often find it embarrassing. However, as our society becomes more multi-cultural, the idea and practice of negotiation is becoming more acceptable.

Negotiation is in fact a form of selling, and is not necessarily only about money or the price of something. In everyday life, without realising, we negotiate with other people several times a day.

Example: A conversation between you and one of your therapists may go like this:

You: Claire, can you work late till 8p.m. instead of 7p.m. next Wednesday? Mrs Jarvis is going on holiday and is desperate for some waxing. (You are trying to sell your request.)

Therapist: Oh, next Wednesday? I've arranged to see my nephew that evening. (She is trying to sell you her excuse.)

You: But I really need you (you are selling your reason), and will appreciate it if you could rearrange another time to see your nephew.

Therapist: OK then, but any chance of finishing an hour earlier on Thursday? (Claire is negotiating.)

You: Of course you can. I'll write it in the book. (You have agreed with the terms of negotiation.)

Example: Two friends want to go out for dinner. One suggests one type of food; the other explains why they should eat another type of food (they are trying to sell their view to each other). After several minutes of talk and reasoning with each other, they hopefully agree on what to eat (they have been negotiating). If in the meantime they have not decided where to eat, then the negotiation will start again on which restaurant they should go to. Each one will try to convince the other that their choice of restaurant is a better one (selling again, this time their choice of restaurant to each other). Neither realises that they have effectively been going through a 'selling' process, through a series of 'negotiations'.

In a typical day, we may negotiate with our partner, taxi driver, newsagent, window cleaner, a waiter, our children, parents, the bank clerk and many more.

As negotiation is a process of selling, the same two skills of **self-confidence** and **communication** are needed for good negotiation.

In your business, most of your negotiation will be with your staff, clients, tradesmen and of course your product suppliers. Negotiation is extremely useful when it comes to having a job done or purchasing products or other essentials for the salon where you can effectively save thousands of pounds.

One of the secrets of good negotiation is to know as much as possible about the position of your opposition (the person you are negotiating with). In the example above, if one of the friends is paying for the dinner, then they are in a better negotiating position.

The following are some examples of a strong negotiating position for a purchaser:

- ☐ The seller has too many of that product left.

- ☐ The seller has cash-flow problems and desperately needs money.

- ☐ The seller is a salesman with a target to reach; he can therefore drop his commission margin dramatically in order to reach his target.

- ☐ The seller's product is reaching its sell-by date.

- ☐ The seller has sold hardly any of these products and wants to get rid of them.

- ☐ The seller's business is closing down.

□ The product is slightly soiled.

□ The seller has a new product or service and wants to promote it (this is where you can even get free samples).

These are rather general points and could apply to any business. If the purchaser knows the facts behind the sale of a product or service, he or she will use this knowledge to negotiate hard and get the best possible deal.

In general, when you need to negotiate, follow the steps below:

1. Research the company you are going to buy from.

2. Find out as much as possible about the person you are going to negotiate with.

3. Look around for the same or similar product and find out who else is selling it and at what price.

4. If possible, find out if what you have been offered is sold to anyone else at a lower price.

5. Find out if the company you are going to deal with is in a good financial position.

6. Get a feel of the going rate for what you want to buy or something as similar to it as possible.

7. Using all the information you have gathered, and using the asking price as your guide, decide on the price which you believe is value for money to you and that you can comfortably afford (your ideal price).

8. Ask the seller what is the best price they can give you.

9. If the price they give you is below your ideal price, you can accept it.

10. If their offer price is above your ideal price, give them the price that you are happy to proceed with and sit and wait for the seller's response.

11. If there is no immediate response, don't chase them; wait until they come back to you. One of three things will now happen:

   – They will accept your offer.

— They will come back with another figure between yours and theirs; in this case you can negotiate further.

— They don't come back to you. This means your offer is way off the mark and you may have to revise your figure. Start the process again from Step 7.

What you need to run a successful salon

Running a successful beauty salon is not just about luck or opening it and hoping for the best. It is not only about a good location, or having a beautifully-decorated place with a good ambience. It is not about being cheap or giving lots of special offers. It is a complex combination of the following:

☐ Good and effective management of time, staff, the salon, your clients and your business.

☐ Thorough understanding of your industry, treatments and products.

☐ Support from your family and friends.

☐ Solid financial position with back-up if and when necessary.

☐ Good location and the right treatments and products for the area.

☐ Strong commitment and self-belief.

☐ Your You Factor.

What could cause disaster

Launching a business, regardless of size or type, can be risky and success is not always guaranteed. Most failures happen during the early years of trading. It is estimated that 20% of new businesses fail within their first year and 50% go bust in the first three years.

These figures are frightening but should not scare you off. By knowing the problems and challenges which lie ahead of you, you can avoid the issues which could potentially destroy your business; and with hard work and following the correct guidelines, your new business can and should be successful.

An excellent source of information for new businesses is the government's business website. Visit www.businesslink.gov.uk

All or any of the following could potentially ruin your chances of having a successful business:

- [ ] Lack of proper planning

- [ ] Poor or inadequate market research

- [ ] Weak financial arrangements

- [ ] Over-ambitious ideas and setting goals too high

- [ ] Taking your eye off the competition

- [ ] Bad choice of treatments and products

- [ ] Pricing products and treatments inappropriately

- [ ] Employing the wrong staff

- [ ] Lack of commitment from you

All the dos for a successful business

- [ ] Analyse your own motivation and level of commitment. Make sure that the reason behind your decision to open a beauty salon is well justified and that you are able to be 100% committed.

- [ ] Take your time, study your market and make all your decisions based on the facts and figures available to you and **not** on excitement and hope.

- [ ] Make sure that you have a proper business plan.

- [ ] Ensure that your finances are well arranged with sufficient margin for the unexpected and over-spending, particularly during the early stages of the business.

- [ ] Surround yourself with positive people and use only well-trained and committed staff. Make sure you have a strong team to work with you.

- [ ] Keep records of everything from day one; without organised record-keeping, management becomes much harder.

- [ ] Make good use of professional people such as a solicitor, a competent accountant and, if necessary, a surveyor. Their advice is often invaluable.

- [ ] Always use recommended and registered tradesmen. Cheap and cheerful normally ends up costing you more in the long run.

- [ ] Be pro-active. Make things happen.

☐ Use appropriate marketing and advertising without wasting thousands of pounds.

☐ Try to be decisive in your actions. Dithering causes doubt in your own belief and in others who work for you.

☐ Keep up with the latest developments in the world of beauty treatments and products. Read trade magazines and visit trade shows regularly.

☐ Memberships of associated trades and professional bodies such as The Guild of Beauty Therapists and BABTAC (British Association of Beauty Therapy and Cosmetology) are very useful as they offer many benefits. Join them.

☐ Make sure your credit rating remains clean.

☐ Be, act and remain professional at all times.

☐ Delegate and divide duties and jobs among your staff.

☐ Ensure that you have comprehensive insurance cover for your business and all your staff.

☐ Make sure that everything is within the law and the regulations and requirements of your local authorities.

☐ Learn the art of negotiation and make sure you always negotiate for the best deal.

☐ Pay your suppliers and creditors on time and keep a professional relationship with them.

☐ Take time off from the business to relax and do what you enjoy doing most.

All the don'ts in your business

☐ Don't get carried away with the excitement and emotion of your new business and don't make hasty decisions.

☐ Don't expect everything to go smoothly at first; there will be many disappointments on the way.

☐ Do not under-estimate the amount of effort and commitment that is needed from you.

□ Don't employ inexperienced staff when you first open. You won't have time to spend with them.

□ Don't be persuaded to buy things that you don't need or you don't want. Choose what is right for you and your business.

□ Do not cut corners. There is no shortcut to success.

□ Don't take your eyes off your competitors. They might catch you by surprise.

□ Don't sit and wait for things to happen. They won't, unless you make them happen.

□ Do not supply people you don't know well or you are not sure about with goods or services on credit.

□ Don't try to do everything yourself. You will get buried under tons of tasks, jobs and paperwork, and you will fail.

□ Don't neglect your health, private life and social life. It will otherwise reduce your efficiency and adversely affect your judgement and management skill.

Making clients love your salon

Finding clients and attracting new ones all the time is hard enough, but keeping them in love with your salon is even harder. The following, although it may sound obvious, will ensure that your clients and customers want to come back to your salon again and again, because they just love the place:

□ Make sure all your treatments are of a high standard and are consistent. Don't give a good treatment – make sure it is a **great treatment**.

□ Offer customer service that goes above and beyond that of others.

□ Choose products and treatments that produce results, not gimmicks.

□ Use only professional and well-trained staff who are confident about what they advise and in what they do.

□ Make sure your salon has that 'personal touch'; make every customer feel they are very special.

□ The first impression is made during the first telephone call or the first visit to your salon. Make sure it is right and it is good.

□ Always make sure your clients are made to feel special when they leave, even if they don't have a treatment or buy anything.

□ Make changes to your reception and displays as regularly as possible. If you don't, the place will look stale.

□ Do not display too many promotions or messages at the same time. This is visual pollution. It confuses clients and will have a negative effect.

□ Pay attention to detail; in your treatments, in the tidiness of the salon and especially in cleanliness and hygiene. It does matter and will make a lot of difference.

□ Maintain a very high standard of cleanliness, hygiene and sterilisation practices.

□ Keep an eye on what's new and hot in the beauty industry, do your research, and if suitable, be the first to offer it to your clients.

□ Remember the names of your clients, their favourite drink and topic of conversation.

□ Make sure you know what your clients want. If you don't know, then ask, and ask again. Don't assume anything.

Finally . . .

Starting your own beauty salon business is going to be one of the most exciting events of your life. It will, however, be stressful, hard work and at times very lonely. It can be compared with climbing a tough mountain; you will need lots of planning and preparation, good health, experience, direction, the right tools and equipment, a first-aid kit and hard work. On the way up you will find many obstacles in your way which you will have to negotiate. You will fall a few times and possibly get hurt. The weather will change: sometimes it will be warm and calm, sometimes it will get cold and turn stormy. At times you will feel lonely and isolated. But eventually, using the skills that you have learned, your hard work and continuous effort, determination and persistence will pay off and you will reach the summit. This is the time that you have longed for, the place that you have dreamed so much about. As you stand on the top and look around, you will experience the most exhilarating feeling. This is when you realise you have made it and that your beauty salon is a success. Happy climbing!

INDEX

A142305